Sing a New Psalm to The Lord

The 23rd Psalm 23 Ways
Songs for the Heart and Beauty for the Soul

Beverly Herbrandson Koester
Photography by Trinity Skiadas

ForwardMoving Publishing
Lisbon Falls, ME, USA

Sing a New Psalm
Published by ForwardMoving Publishing, Lisbon Falls, ME, USA
© 2014 by Beverly Herbrandson Koester
All rights reserved. Published 2014
2 3 4 5 6 7 8 9
Printed in the United States of America

Photography by Trinity Skiadas
Cover and interior layout and design by Beverly Koester

All Scripture quotations are taken from the King James Version Bible

100% of the profit from the sale of this book will be placed in a scholarship fund to assist students attending Christian schools

Acknowledgments: Thanks to Rod Herbrandson for the deer and the eagle photographs, and to all who assisted in proofreading and editing.

You can obtain more copies of this book at
www.forwardmoving.com

ISBN-13: 978-0-9905175-0-4

Table of Contents

	Introduction	8
1st	Joy	10
2nd	Peace	14
3rd	Confidence	18
4th	Guide	22
5th	Compassionate Savior	26
6th	Father	30
7th	Father, but I have Rebelled	34
8th	Crucified and Risen Savior	38
9th	Redeemer	42
10th	Strength	46
11th	Creator	50
12th	Comfort	54
13th	Life	58
14th	Almighty God	62
15th	Forgiveness (Words)	66
16th	Youth	70
17th	Old Age	74
18th	Rock	78
19th	Counselor	82
20th	Sovereign God (Tragedy)	86
21st	Light	90
22nd	Refuge	94
23rd	Judge	98

Using this Book

It is our hope and prayer that you find this book a blessing. Take time to feed your soul on each picture of God's creation. Use the psalms as study outlines, as Bible marking guides, and as tools to assist in locating encouraging verses.

Choose a psalm and dig into it. Research the topic. Look up the references. Find more and even better verses to back up each idea. Journal your thoughts.

The psalms are designed to be read aloud. Read them for family worship. Share them with your children, your parents, and your friends. Use them to springboard discussion in your small study group.

The Musical Notes

The musical notes used throughout this book are actually the first two measures of the hymn, "Sing a New Song to the Lord," by David G. Wilson.

Dedicated

To our dear friend, Donna Cooper, and to the memory of her late husband, Andy, who, despite their illnesses, assisted in testing the use of these psalms in small group study.

The 23rd Psalm

The Lord is my shepherd; I shall not want.

♪ He maketh me to lie down in green pastures: he leadeth me beside the still waters.

♪ He restoreth my soul: he leadeth me in the paths of righteousness for his name's sake.

♪ Yea, though I walk through the valley of the shadow of death, I will fear no evil: for thou art with me; thy rod and thy staff they comfort me.

♪ Thou preparest a table before me in the presence of mine enemies: thou anointest my head with oil; my cup runneth over.

♪ Surely goodness and mercy shall follow me all the days of my life: and I will dwell in the house of the Lord for ever.

Introduction

∽ Introduction ∽

"The Lord is my shepherd, I shall not want. He makes me to lie down in green pastures. He leads m e . . z . z . z . z z z   zzz."

For years I recited the 23rd Psalm as I drifted off to sleep, then one night something different happened. I tried imagining walking with the shepherd. I had no trouble lying down in green pastures, for I like to lie in flowery meadows and watch fluffy clouds. I had a bit more difficulty with the still waters, though. I don't drink from ponds. I do have memories of zebra, gazelles, and even elephants drinking from watering holes, but I have never seen a sheep drink.

By the time my thoughts got this far, I was not very dreamy. So I asked myself just how the 23rd Psalm would be written today. The Lord is my . . . Father. Yes! I could relate to that. I have no trouble remembering my dad's twinkle when he had a humorous story to tell me. I recall comforting arms, evenings of counseling, and gifts of love. Yes, I could relate to the Lord being my father. Wide awake, I began writing in my head, and, before I finally slept, the first new psalm was composed.

Writing the Heart Songs

I set up some fun rules, which I loosely followed. These psalms are divided into six verses, roughly following the pattern of the 23rd. For many of the psalms, I did a word study using mostly verses containing the theme word or words (see "Father," "Counselor," and "Compassion"), for some I did a theme study (see "Peace,"

"Redeemer," and "Sovereign"), and for a few I extrapolated and condensed the thoughts from specific verses or chapters (see "Crucified and Risen Savior," and "I Have Rebelled"). For these, you will wish to read the entire chapter as I did not footnote specific verses. Each new psalm finishes, as does the 23rd, with some reference to our eternal home which, amazingly, always showed up in every category!

The Footnotes

Sometimes a scripture verse is used more than once. When this is the case, the same footnote number is used. Note the paragraph taken from the psalm, "Guide":

> Surely, my Lord is leading me to His everlasting home,[18] where He will give me to drink of the waters of life,[19] shower me with treasures,[20] and wipe away my tears.[19] ([18]*Psalm 139:23, 24.* [19]*Revelation 7:17.* [20]*Proverbs 8:20, 21.*)

You see that Revelation 7:17 is referenced twice, using the same footnote (number 19). Please do not let yourself get confused with the numbers that are out of sequence.

Songs for Your Heart

These psalms are songs for the heart to sing.[1] Their quiet melody will bring comfort and encouragement, inspire deeper study into the wonderful Word of God, and increase love for and trust in our Lord and Savior, Jesus Christ. ([1]*Ephesians 5:19.*)

O sing unto the Lord a new song; for he hath done marvellous things: His right hand, and His holy arm, hath gotten Him the victory. **Psalm 98:1**

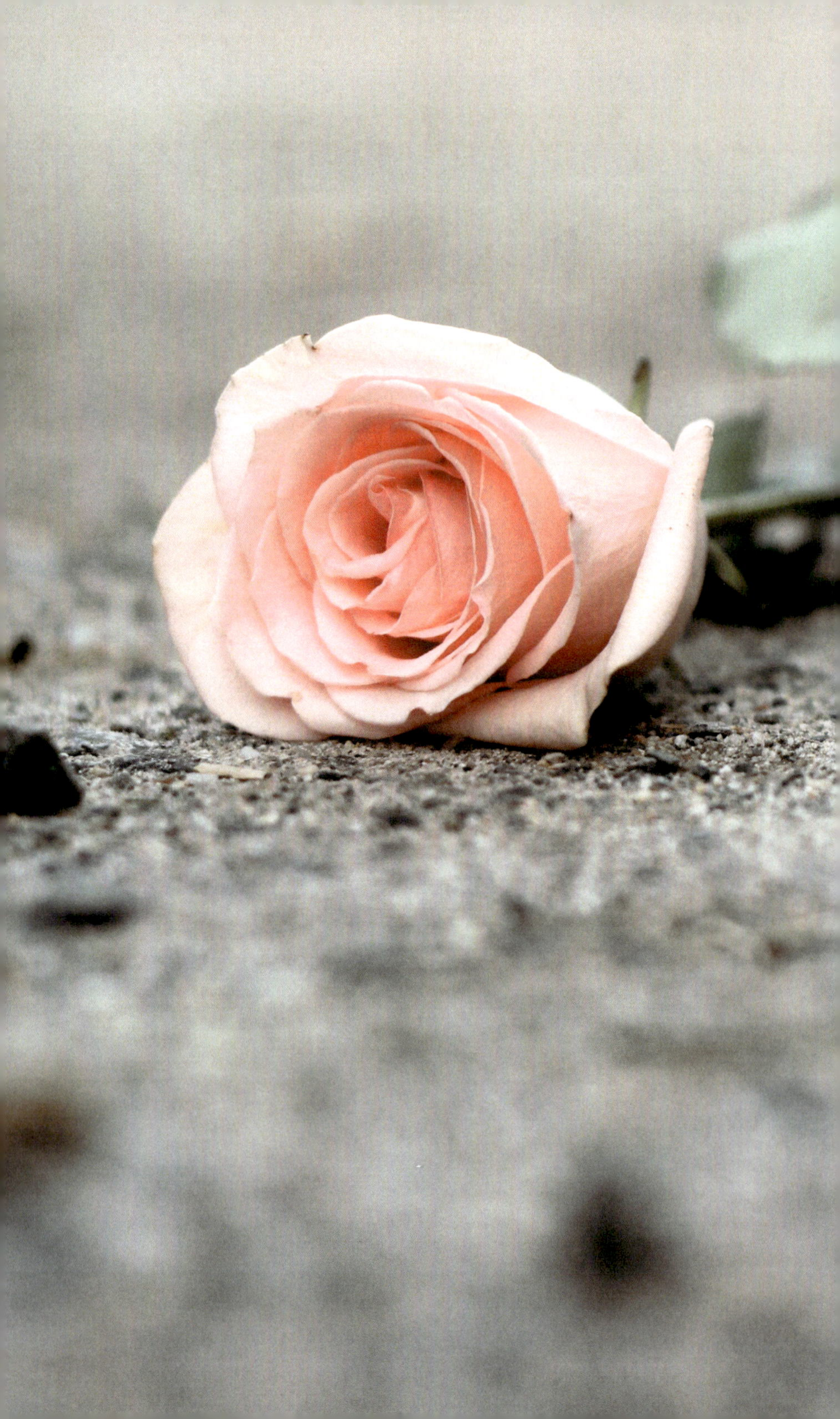

The Lord is My Joy

~ Joy ~

The Lord is my joy;[1] sorrow and mourning shall flee away![2] *([1]Habakkuk 3:17, 18. [2]Isaiah 51:11.)*

♪ I rejoice, because He feeds me with His words[3] and provides water from the well of His salvation.[4] I am His joy,[5] and He is mine.[6] *([3]Jeremiah 15:16. [4]Isaiah 12:3. [5]Zephaniah 3:17. [6]Psalm 16:11.)*

♪ He leads me on the path of life. His presence lights my way[7] and fills me with exceeding joy.[6] When I stumble, He lifts me up. He not only restores my joy,[8] but teaches me how to retain it by abiding in His love.[9] *([7]Psalm 43:3, 4. [8]Psalm 51:9-13. [9]John 15:10-12.)*

♪ When trials come[10] and the joy of my heart is ceased,[11] His joy becomes my strength.[12] I weep all night, but He has mercy upon me and restores my joy in the morning.[13] *([10]1 Peter 4:12-14. [11]Lamentations 5:15. [12]Nehemiah 8:10. [13]Psalm 30:5, 10, 11; Jeremiah 31:13.)*

♪ When my brother turns against me, my Lord is my defense.[14] He lifts my head above my enemies; therefore, I offer Him sacrifices of joy and songs of praise.[15] When I speak of the joy of my salvation,[16] sinners are converted and my Lord is pleased.[8] *([14]Psalm 5:11, 12. [15]Psalm 27:6. [16]Psalm 35:27, 28.)*

♪ Surely joy and gladness shall follow me all the days of my life,[17] and soon He will, with exceeding joy,[18] welcome me into His kingdom[19] where there are pleasures forevermore![6] *([17]Isaiah 35:10. [18]Jude 24. [19]Matthew 25:21, 23.)*

The joy of the Lord is my strength. **Nehemiah 8:10**

The Lord is My Peace

~ PEACE ~

The Lord is my peace;[1] I stand fearless in the midst of troubles.[2] (*[1]John 14:27. [2]Deuteronomy 20:1-4.*)

♪ When my soul is melted, I cry unto the Lord, and He calms my storm.[3] (*[3]Psalm 107:26-30; Mark 4:39.*)

♪ Sometimes I burn with an inner fire.[4] I want to lash out—to spew out my feelings,[5] my anger,[6] my sorrow,[7] my human opinion.[8] Then I cry out in silent tears, "Lord, keep my tongue from sinning."[4] He hears and gives me peace that passes understanding.[9] I recover my strength and go forward.[4] (*[4]Psalm 39:1-13. [5]Exodus 14:14. [6]Romans 12:17, 18. [7]Nehemiah 8:10, 11. [8]1 Corinthians 14:29-34. [9]Philippians 4:7; Malachi 2:6.*)

♪ Let the storm rage, I shall remain calm.[3] Let sorrow come, I shall rejoice.[10] Let persecution assail, I shall patiently wait upon the

Lord.[11] Let troubles overtake me, I shall be comforted.[12] Let famine ravish, I shall be satisfied. Let evil surround me, I shall hold my peace and neither be ashamed[13] or troubled,[14] for my hope is in the Lord![15] *([10]John 16:20-22. [11]1 Peter 2:20, 21; Psalm 37:34-40. [12]Psalm 71:20, 21. [13]Psalm 37:19. [14]John 14:1-3. [15]Zephaniah 1:7, 8.)*

♪ As long as my mind is stayed on Him, I have perfect peace.[16] *([16]Isaiah 26:3.)*

♪ Surely my days shall be filled with an abundance of peace, and my end shall be in the new earth[17] where there shall be peace forevermore.[18] *([17]Psalm 37:11. [18]Isaiah 66:12, 22, 23.)*

Thou wilt keep him in perfect peace, whose mind is stayed on Thee: because he trusteth in Thee. ISAIAH 26:3

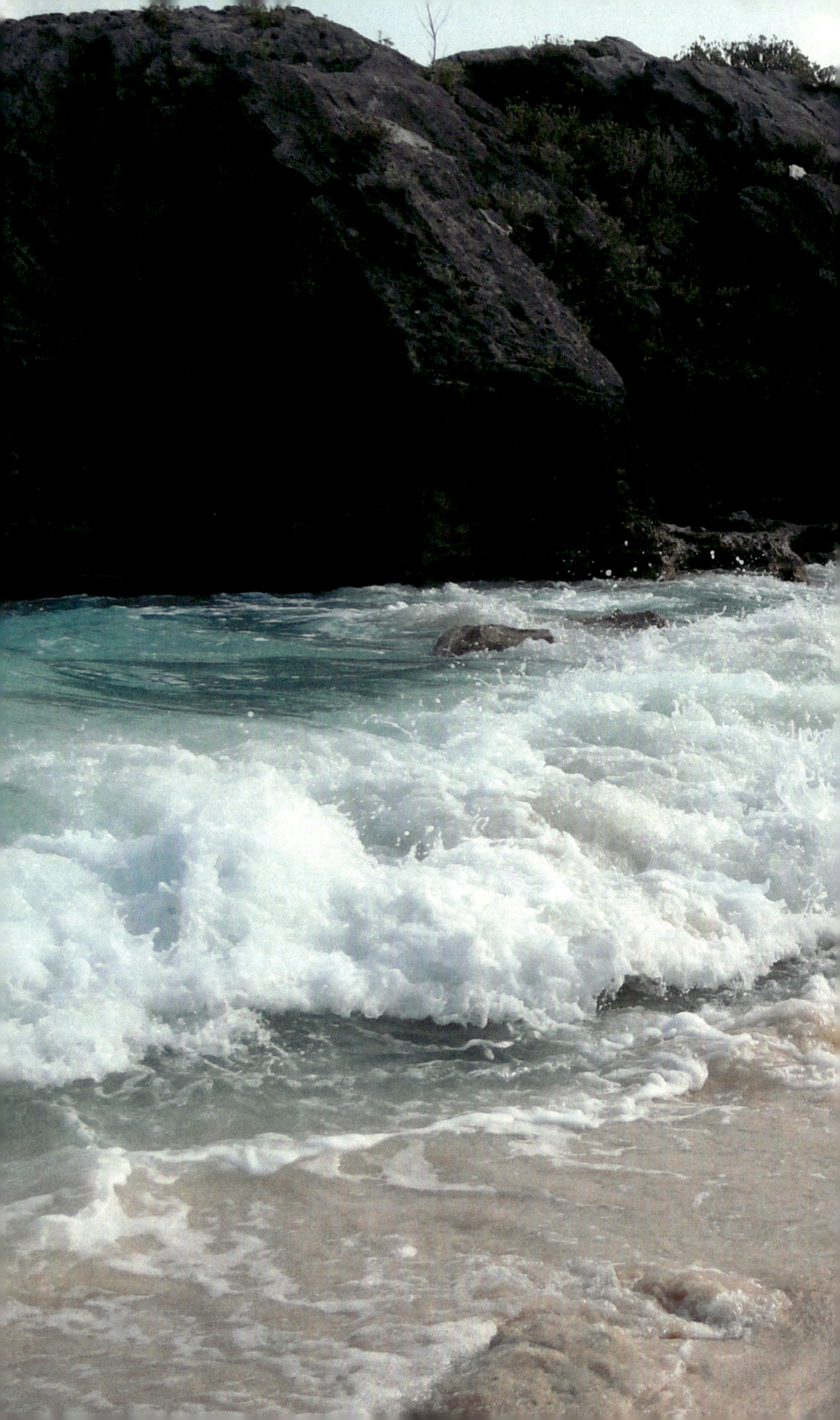

The Lord is My Confidence

◈ CONFIDENCE ◈

The Lord is my confidence; I have no fear, for He walks with me.[1] (*[1]Psalm 118:6-18.*)

♪ My friends, and even my family, have let me down, but I am not stranded. I confidently turn to my Lord, and He provides my needs.[2] (*[2]Micah 7:4-7.*)

♪ Because He laid down His life[3] for my salvation,[4] takes away my shame,[5] and gives me eternal life, He has a vested interest in my future. I have confidence[6] He will keep me from evil, discipline me when I need it,[1] bring conviction to my heart,[7] and enable me to please Him.[8] (*[3]1 John 3:16. [4]Psalm 65:5-8. [5]1 John 2:28. [6]Philippians 1:6. [7]1 John 3:18-21. [8]2 Thessalonians 3:3-5.*)

♪ I face the challenges of the day and the fears of the night with songs[1] of rejoicing.[4] I sleep in peace[9] and wait out storms in quietness,[10] for my Lord, in whom I have confidence, formed the mountains and controls the seas.[1] I face the dangers around[11] me in His name, for He is my strength and my salvation.[1] *([9]Proverbs 3:24-26. [10]Isaiah 30:15. [11]Psalm 27:3-4.)*

♪ I can even take joyfully the loss of everything I own,[13] for my hope is firm,[14] and my reward is sure.[13] *([13]Hebrews 10:34-37. [14]Hebrews 3:6.)*

♪ Surely my Lord shall come[14] to take me to Himself, where I shall dwell in His house, be showered with His goodness, and behold His beauty[11]—forever![15] *([15]1 John 5:13-15.)*

The steps of a good man are ordered by the Lord: and He delighteth in his way. Though he fall, he shall not be utterly cast down: for the Lord uphooldeth him with His hand. Psalm 37:23, 24

The Lord is My Guide

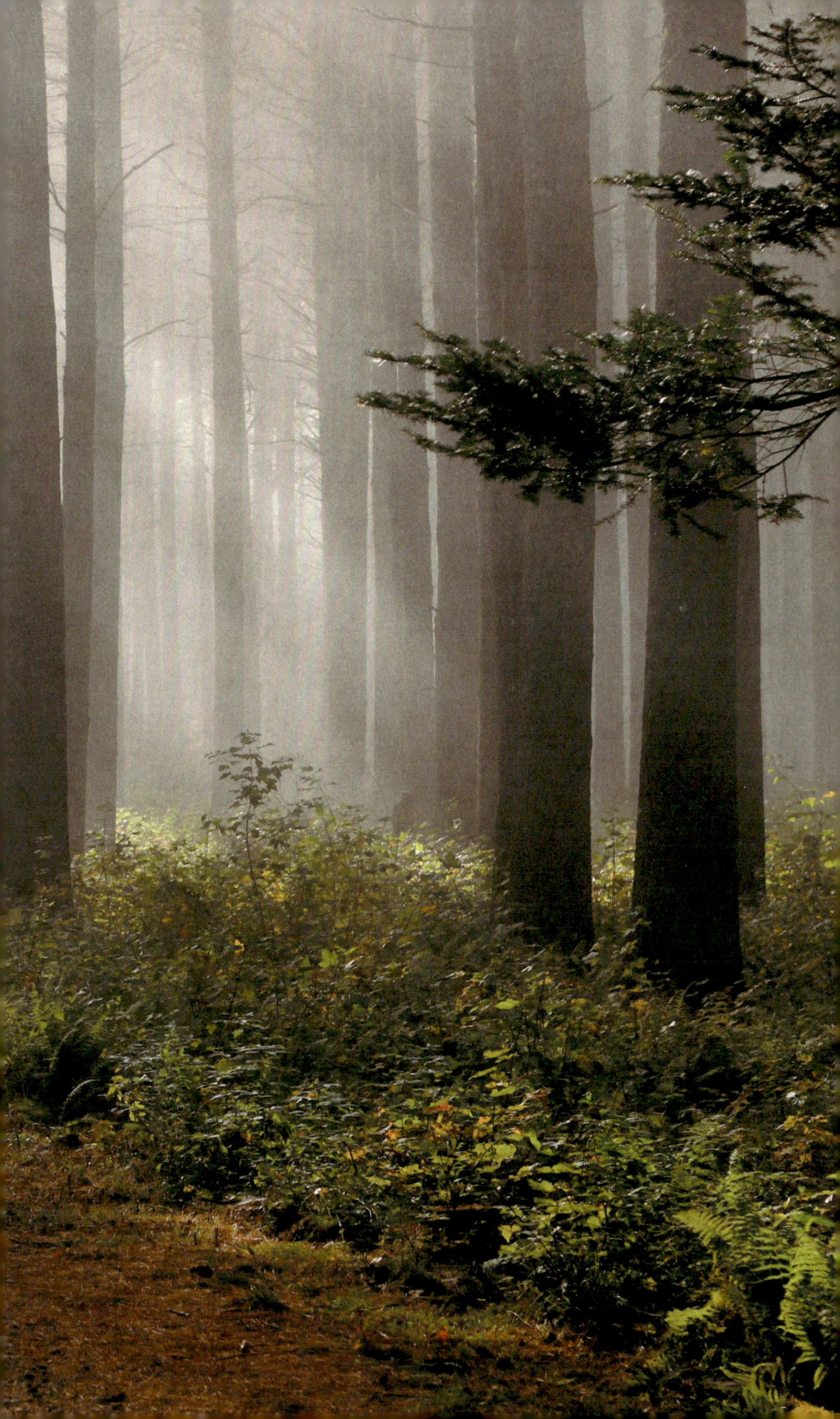

~ GUIDE ~

The Lord is my gentle, very capable, all-powerful Guide;[1] I shall follow in the path He directs.[2] *([1]Isaiah 40:10-13. [2]Proverbs 3:5, 6; Isaiah 42:16.)*

♪ His path leads me to live an honest, godly, quiet and peaceable life,[3] and ends in His presence, where I will have great joy and endless pleasures.[4] *([3]1 Timothy 2:2. [4]Psalm 16:9, 11.)*

♪ He guides me with His eye[5] and provides me with a map,[6] a light,[7] protection,[8] and a helping hand.[9] He is my strength in the face of danger,[10] my shelter from the elements, and my comfort[11] in death.[12] *([5]Psalm 32:8. [6]Psalm 119:105. [7]Psalm 43:3; Proverbs 4:18. [8]Psalm 91:11, 12. [9]Psalm 139:9, 10. [10]Psalm 31:3, 4. [11]Isaiah 49:10-13. [12]Psalm 23:4.)*

♪ When my foot slips,[13] or I wander from the path and bring disaster upon myself, I come to Him in tears. He reaches out in tender mercies and lovingkindness, forgives my sins,[14] and leads me back to the straight way.[15] *([13]Psalm 37:23, 24. [14]Psalm 25:4-7, 10-11. [15]Jeremiah 31:8, 9; Nehemiah 9:18-21; Matthew 7:13, 14.)*

♪ When my heart is overwhelmed, He draws me to Himself[16] and reminds me that He has a plan for my future.[17] *([16]Psalm 61:2. [17]Jeremiah 29:11-14.)*

♪ Surely, my Lord is leading me to His everlasting home,[18] where He will give me to drink of the waters of life,[19] shower me with treasures[20] and wipe away my tears.[19] *([18]Psalm 139:23, 24. [19]Revelation 7:17. [20]Proverbs 8:20, 21.)*

Trust in the Lord with all thine heart; and lean not unto thine own understanding. In all thy ways acknowledge Him, and He shall direct thy paths.
Proverbs 3:5-6

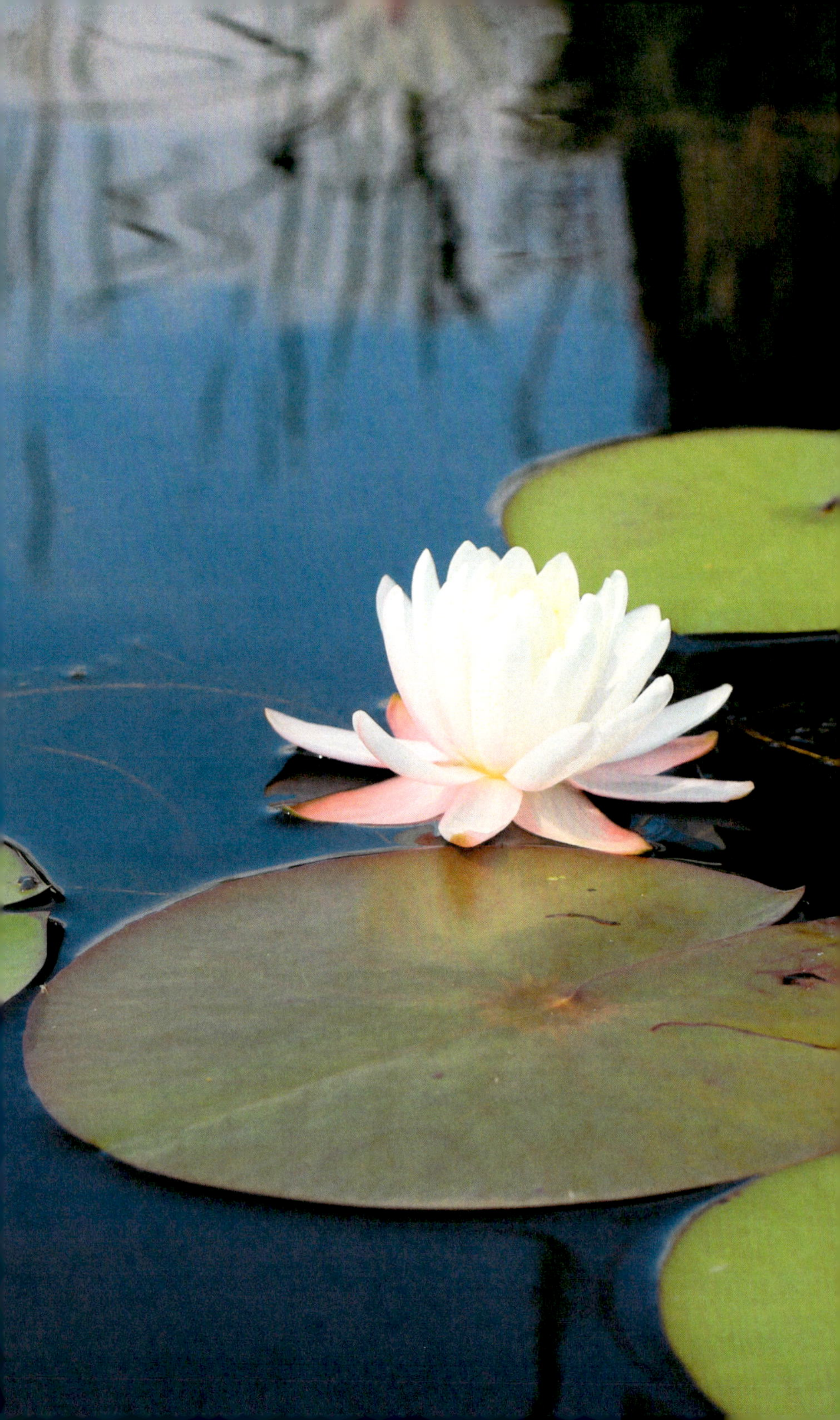

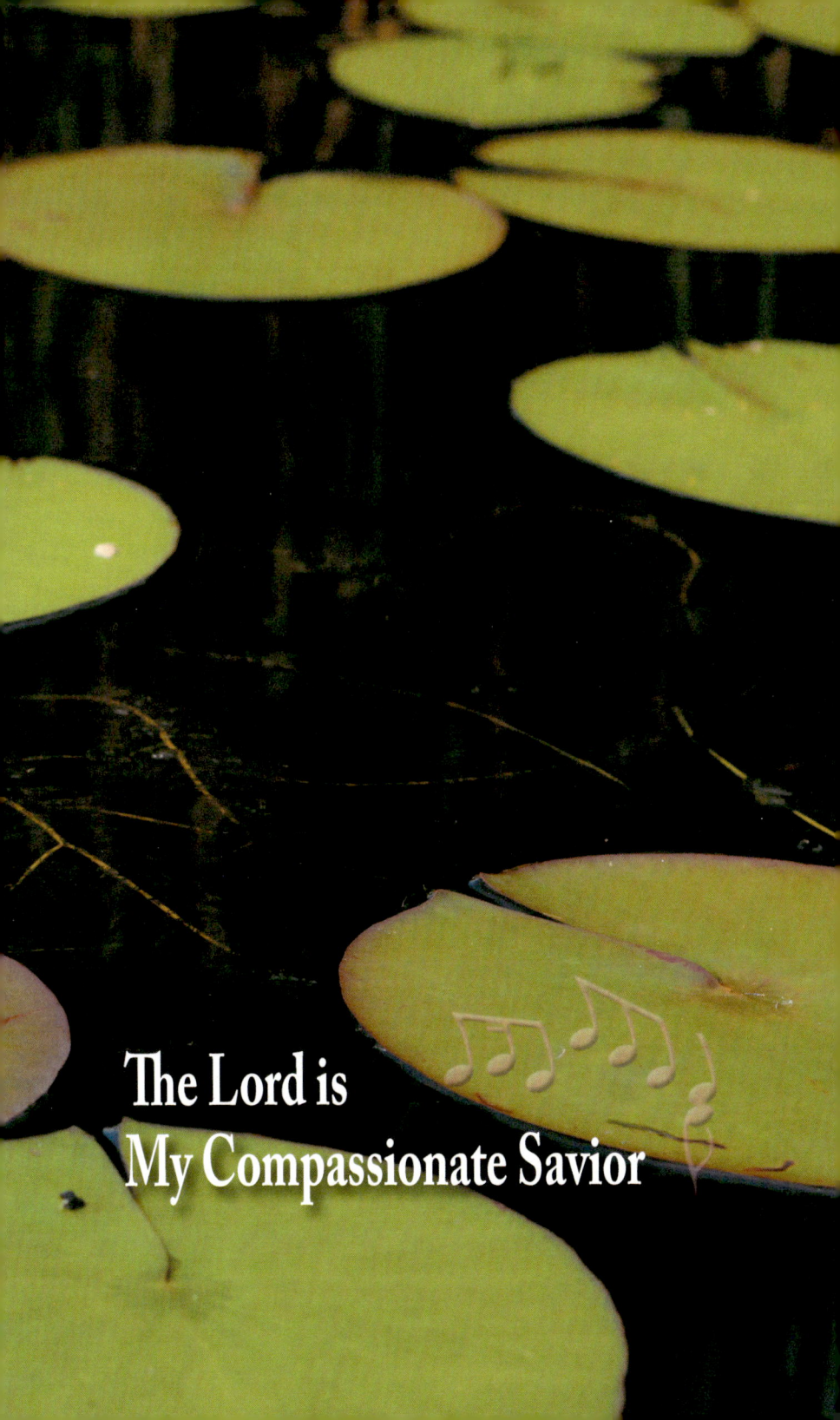

The Lord is My Compassionate Savior

~ COMPASSION ~

The Lord is my compassionate Savior; I am but flesh, and He understands.[1] *([1]Psalm 78:37-39.)*

♪ He pardons my iniquity, overlooks my faults and subdues my strong passions.[2] He tenderly cares for me[3] and takes pity upon me[4] when I am overwhelmed with troubles.[5] He puts food on my table[6] and wealth in[7] and out of[8] my pocket. *([2]Micah 7:18-19. [3]Psalm 145:8-12. [4]Ezekiel 16:5, 6. [5]Lamentations 3:22, 32. [6]Psalm 111:4, 5. [7]Psalm 112:3, 4. [8]Hebrews 10:34.)*

♪ When He came to this earth and made Himself one of us, His suffering gave Him a first-hand understanding of my human nature.[9] *([9]Hebrews 4:15, 16; 5:1-8.)*

♪ The Lord is full of compassion not only towards me but for all His children,[10] His people,[11] His saints,[3] and even towards those who don't yet know Him.[12] Since everyone is graven upon the palms of His hands,[10] His mercy, compassion, and goodness extend to all[3] who will not turn away from Him.[13] His compassionate desire to rescue souls[14] from eternal death[15] knows no cultural barriers.[16] He will not, however, push beyond walls of rebellion[17] or defiance.[13] *([10]Isaiah 49:15-16. [11]Jeremiah 12:14. [12]Mark 6:34-42; Matthew 20:30-34. [13]2 Chronicles 30:7-9. [14]2 Chronicles 36:14-16; Matthew 9:36-38. [15]Psalm 86:14, 15; John 3:16. [16]Luke10:29-37. [17]Deuteronomy 13:17, 18.)*

♪ His compassion dispels my darkness, inspires a compassionate spirit within me, and empowers me to help others.[18] *([18]1 Peter 3:8-9.)*

♪ Surely compassion and mercy[5] shall follow me to the ends of the earth,[19] and I have, in Heaven, a blessed and everlasting inheritance.[18] *([19]Deuteronomy 30:3-4.)*

It is of the Lord's mercies that we are not consumed, because His compassions fail not. They are new every morning. **LAMENTATIONS 3:22, 23**

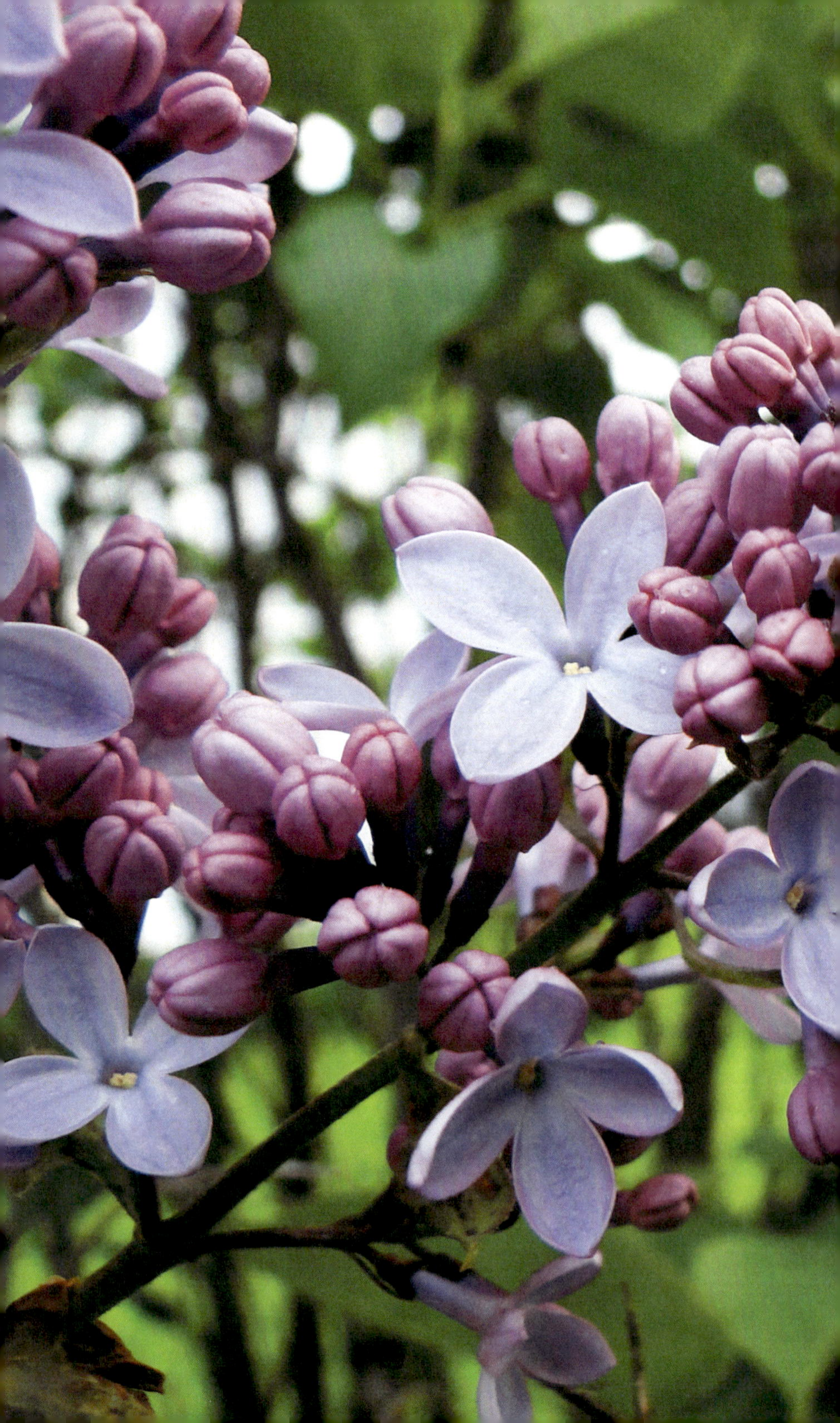

The Lord is My Father

~·Father·~

The Lord is my Father;[1] I shall be called by His everlasting[2] name![3] *([1]Isaiah 64:8; Isaiah 9:6; Romans 8:15-17. [2]Isaiah 63:16. [3]Revelation 22:4.)*

♪ He provides all my needs. I eat His bread,[4] drink from His cup[5] and wear His clothes.[6] He showers me with good gifts.[7] When I have my priorities straight[8] and want to bless others,[9] He actually opens His storehouse of treasures to me.[10] *([4]Matthew 6:9-11, 25-26. [5]Matthew 20:23. [6]Luke 15:22. [7]James 1:17; Luke 11:11-13. [8]Malachi 3:10. [9]Luke 12:31-34. [10]Matthew 6:32-34.)*

♪ He knows me from the inside[11] out,[12] and when I run to Him, crying,[13] He takes my hand[14] and gently leads me where I will not stumble.[13] When I disobey, He forgives me[15] and disciplines[16] me with lovingkindness.[17] He takes pity upon me[18] and comforts me[19] with the Holy Spirit.[20] *([11]Matthew 6:18. [12]Matthew 10:29-31; Matthew 6:8. [13]Jeremiah 31:9. [14]Isaiah 41:13; John 10:25-29. [15]1 John 1:9-2:1. [16]Revelation 3:19-21. [17]Psalms 89:30-33; Proverbs 3:12. [18]Psalms 103:13. [19]Colossians 2:2, 3. [20]John 14:26.)*

♪ When I am harassed by others, He stands up for me[21] and gives me courage and strength[22] to keep going. He is always there when I need Him.[23] *([21]Matthew 18:10, 11. [22]Psalms 27:10-14. [23]John 16:32, 33.)*

♪ My Father knows everything. I treasure His wisdom[19] and hang on His every Word.[24] In fact, my Father can do anything![25] I love to be with Him.[26] I want to be just like Him.[27] *([24]John 1:14; John 6:57, 63; Psalm 119:9-16. [25]Ephesians 3:14-20. [26]1 John 1:3, 4. [27]1 John 3:1-3.)*

♪ Surely He shall be faithful and merciful[8] to me and my children,[29] and soon He will take me home to be with Him for eternity.[30] *([28]Psalms 89:24. [29]Psalms 103:17, 19. [30]John 14:1-3.)*

Behold, what manner of love the Father hath bestowed upon us, that we should be called the sons of God. 1 JOHN 3:1

The Lord is My Father, but I Have Rebelled

~ I Have Rebelled* ~

The Lord is my Father, but I have rebelled.[1]
(*[1]Isaiah 1:2.*)

♪ He nourished me and brought me up. He clothed me in costly apparel and arrayed me with fine jewels, but I was unthankful and wasted His blessings in riotous living. I fed my selfish desires with the food He provided.[2]
(*[2]Ezekiel 16:10-20; Romans 1:21; Luke 15:11-13.*)

♪ He hid His face when I demanded more blessings[3] and left me to the consequences of my choices.[4] He never stopped loving me. Although I broke His heart, He never gave up on me.[5] He pled with me to turn from my willful ways.[6] He promised to forgive all my rebellion and to give me a fresh start.[7] (*[3]Isaiah 1:14-15. [4]Ezekiel 16:35-43; Luke 15:14. [5]Jeremiah 31:3, 4. [6]Isaiah 1:16-20. [7]Luke 15:22.*)

♪ When I was at my lowest, I came to my senses.[8] I was drawn by His lovingkindness,[5] ashamed of my behavior, and humbled by His love. How could I have treated Him so? My heart is changed. I weep in repentance,[9] I weep for joy. I weep in His arms.¹⁰ (⁸*Luke 15:17.* ⁹*Ezekiel 16:60- 63; Jeremiah 31:9, 19, 33.* ¹⁰*Luke 15:20; Deuteronomy 33:27-29.*)

♪ He turned His hand again towards me,¹¹ rescued me from a power I couldn't resist,¹² restored what was lost,¹¹ and placed His robe¹³ of righteousness¹⁴ upon my shoulders¹³ and gave me a new heart.¹⁵ (¹¹*Isaiah 1:25, 26; Joel 2:25, 26.* ¹²*Jeremiah 31:11.* ¹³*Luke 15:21-24.* ¹⁴*Isaiah 61:10. Jeremiah 31:33*)

♪ Surely I am now satisfied.¹⁵ My father and I are reconciled,¹⁶ and He is, right now, preparing a welcome-home party.¹⁷ (¹⁵*Jeremiah 31:14, 25.* ¹⁶*Colossians 1:19-21.* ¹⁷*Luke 15:23, 24; Revelation 3:20, 21.*)

An expanded study of Isaiah 1; Ezekiel 16; Jeremiah 31; and Luke 15:11-32

Let the wicked forsake his way. . . and let him return unto the Lord, and He will have mercy upon him. Isaiah 55:7

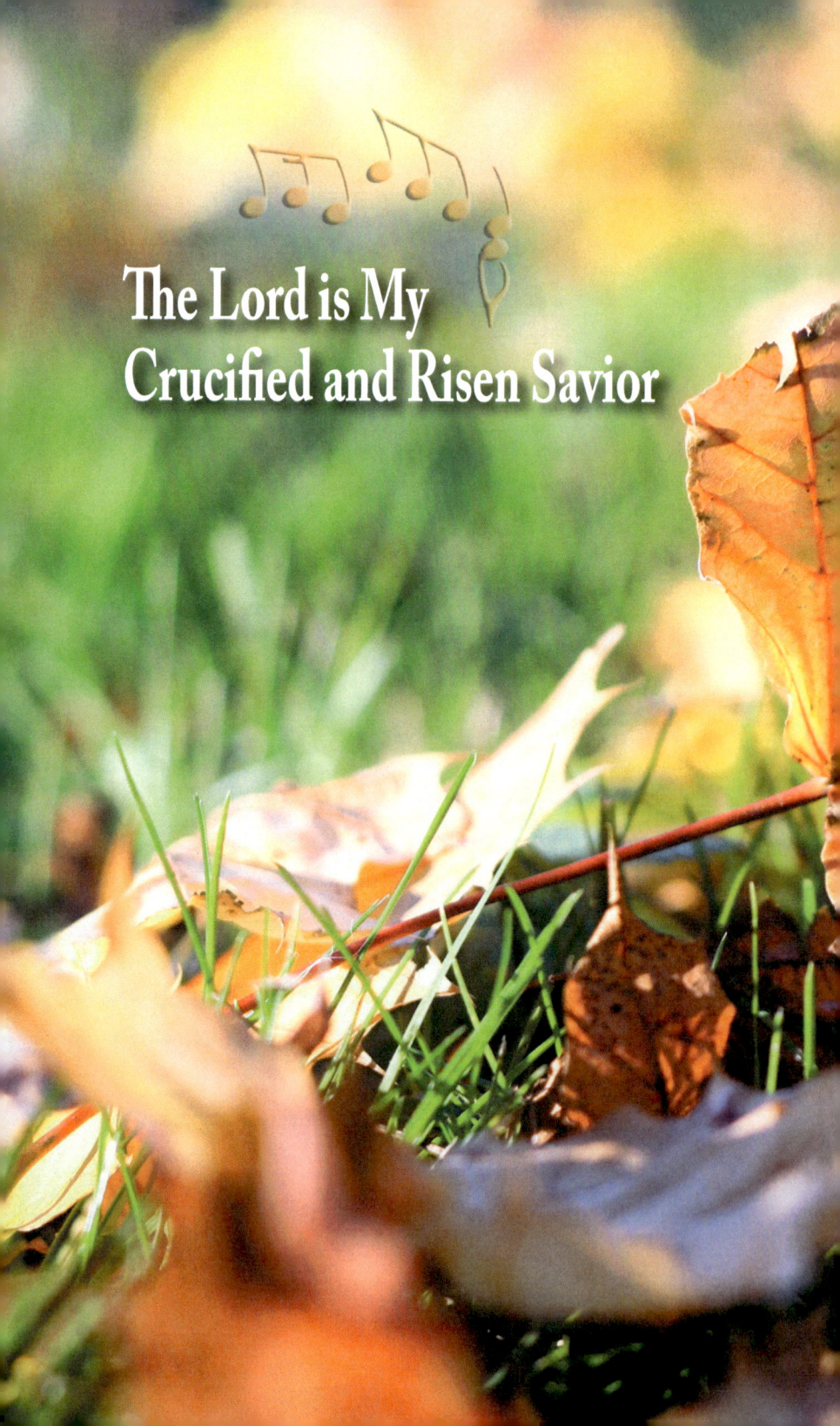

The Lord is My Crucified and Risen Savior

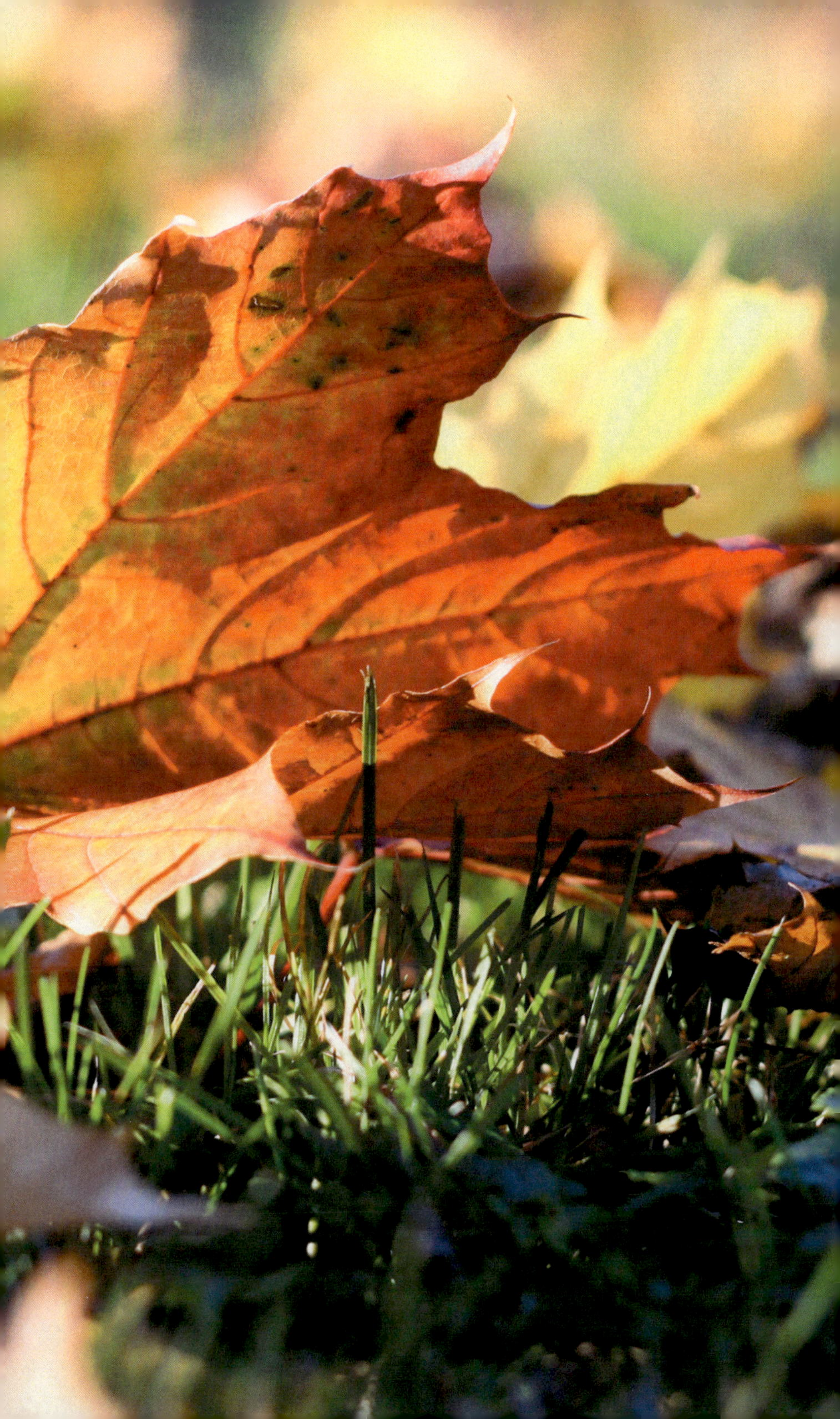

❧ Crucified and Risen Savior*

The Lord is my crucified and risen[1] Savior;[2] He gave Himself for me because He loves me.[3] (*[1] Corinthians 15:20, 21; Philippians 2:8. [2]Acts 4:12. [3]Galatians 2:20.*)

♪ He does not condemn me for my sins, though they are many.[4] Instead, He overcame sin[5] in my stead and thus condemned sin itself. He suffered the penalty that was mine,[6] washed me in His blood,[7] reconciled me through the cross,[8] and filled me with His Spirit. He cast my sins into the depths of the sea[9] and forgot them.[10] (*[4]Luke 7:47. [5]Revelation 3:21. [6]Hebrews 10:10-12, 17. [7]Revelation 1:5. [8]Colossians 1:20. [9]Micah 7:19. [10]Hebrews 10:17.*)

♪ My Lord knows I am weak and sold under sin,[11] so He sent[12] His Spirit to live within me, change my nature, empower me to conquer evil, and help me live His life of righteousness. Although I still find myself doing what I don't want to,[11] I am not condemned.[13] I am picked up,[14] put back on my feet,[15] and, once again, justified. After all, my crucified and risen

Savior is, even now, at the right hand of God, making intercession for me. ([11]Romans 7:14, 15. [12]John 14:26. [13]Romans 7:24-8:1. [14]Psalm 40:2. [15]Psalm 37:23, 24.)

♪ The path I walk is fraught with tribulation, distress, persecution, famine, nakedness, peril, and sword, but He turns all this into my good.[16] ([16]1 Corinthians 4:7-10.)

♪ When God is for me, nothing and no one can be against me, and nothing, absolutely nothing, can separate me from the love of God.[17] ([17]Job 13:15, Job 1:21, 22.)

♪ Surely I face every day with the patient hope that someday my groaning[18] will be replaced with rejoicing,[19] and I shall have glorious freedom. ([18]2 Corinthians 5:4-9. [19]Psalm 126:1, 5.)

* An expanded study of Romans chapter 8. Specific references to verses in chapter 8 are not noted.

If God be for us, who can be against us? ROMANS 8:31

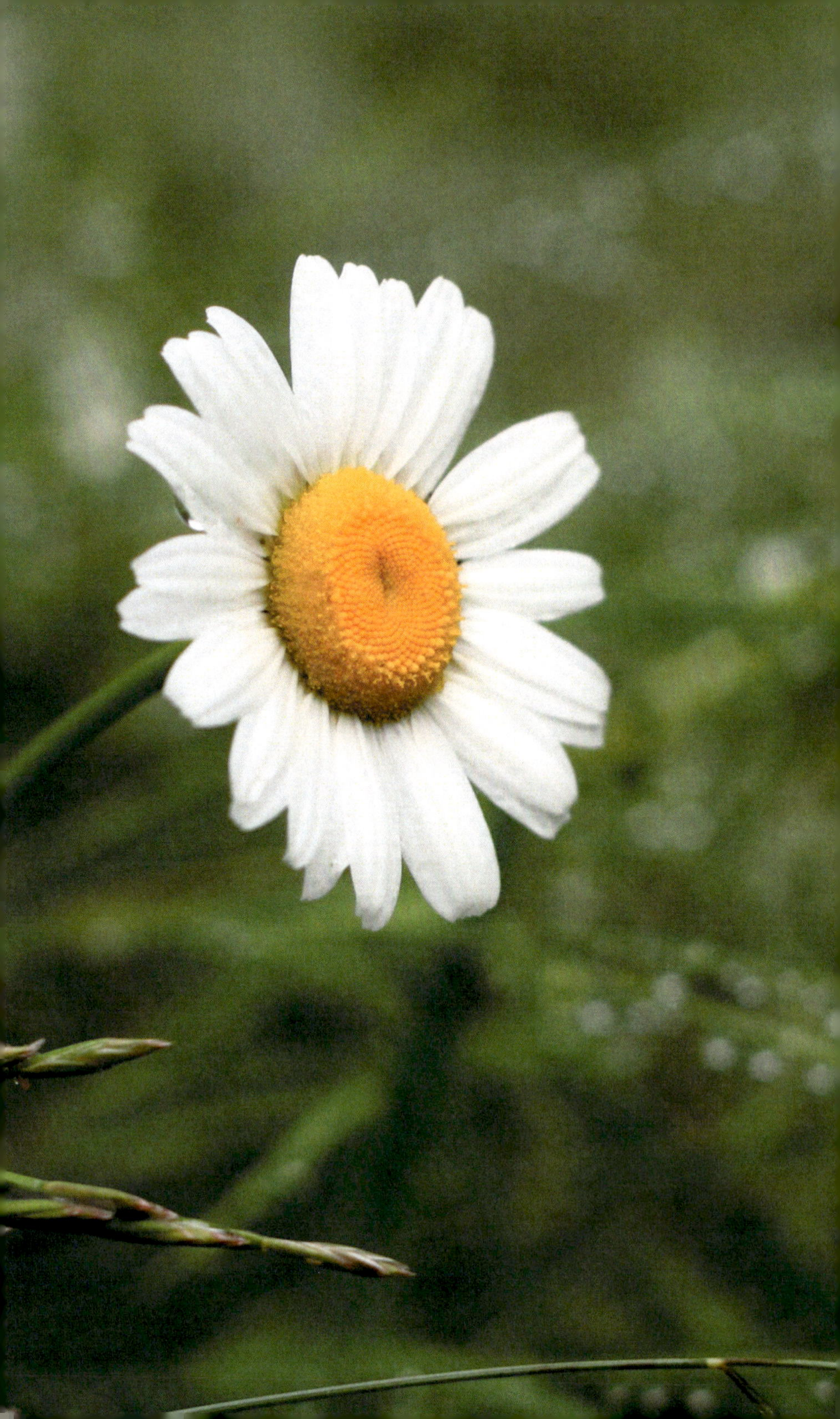

The Lord is My Redeemer

~ REDEEMER ~

The Lord is my Redeemer;[1] I will rejoice in my salvation.[2] (*[1]Isaiah 41:14. [2]Psalm 13:5, 6.*)

♪ He knocks at my door[3] at breakfast time,[4] and I invite Him in. We eat honey[5] on the bread of life[6] and drink sweet wine[7] while we visit.[8] (*[3]Revelation 3:20. [4]Proverbs 8:17. [5]Psalm 119:103. [6]John 6:47-48. [7]1 Corinthians 11:25-26. [8]1 Corinthians 10:16. Note: The word "communion" comes from the Greek word meaning " fellowship.")*

♪ My Redeemer is strong; the Lord of hosts is His name. He is my advocate[9] and financial advisor.[10] He has done great and bountiful things for me, and I am glad.[11] (*[9]Jeremiah 50:34. [10]Isaiah 48:17. [11]Psalm 126:1-3.*)

♪ Although I wandered from my Lord,[12] my Maker,[13] He set me free,[11] redeemed me, and called me His child.[14] I was so overwhelmed[15] with His everlasting kindness[13] that I turned from my transgression[16] to the path that He directs.[10] I go forward[17] in the strength He gives me.[18] (*[12]1 Peter 2:25. [13]Isaiah 54:5, 8. [14]Galatians 4:5. [15]Psalm 116:1, 12, 13. [16]Isaiah*

59:20. [17]*Exodus 14:15.* [18]*Psalm 19:14.*)

♪ I know my Redeemer lives, and though the worm destroys my flesh,[19] He will someday, swallow up death in victory. Then I will declare, "This is my Lord. I have waited for Him. He has saved me. I will be glad and rejoice in His salvation."[20] *([19]Job 19:25-26. [20]Isaiah 25:8-9.)*

♪ Surely mercy and truth have met together, righteousness and peace have kissed each other,[21] and I shall look upon the face[19] of my Redeemer forever. *([21]Psalm 85:10.)*

I know that my Redeemer liveth, and that He shall stand at the latter day upon the earth. JOB 19:25

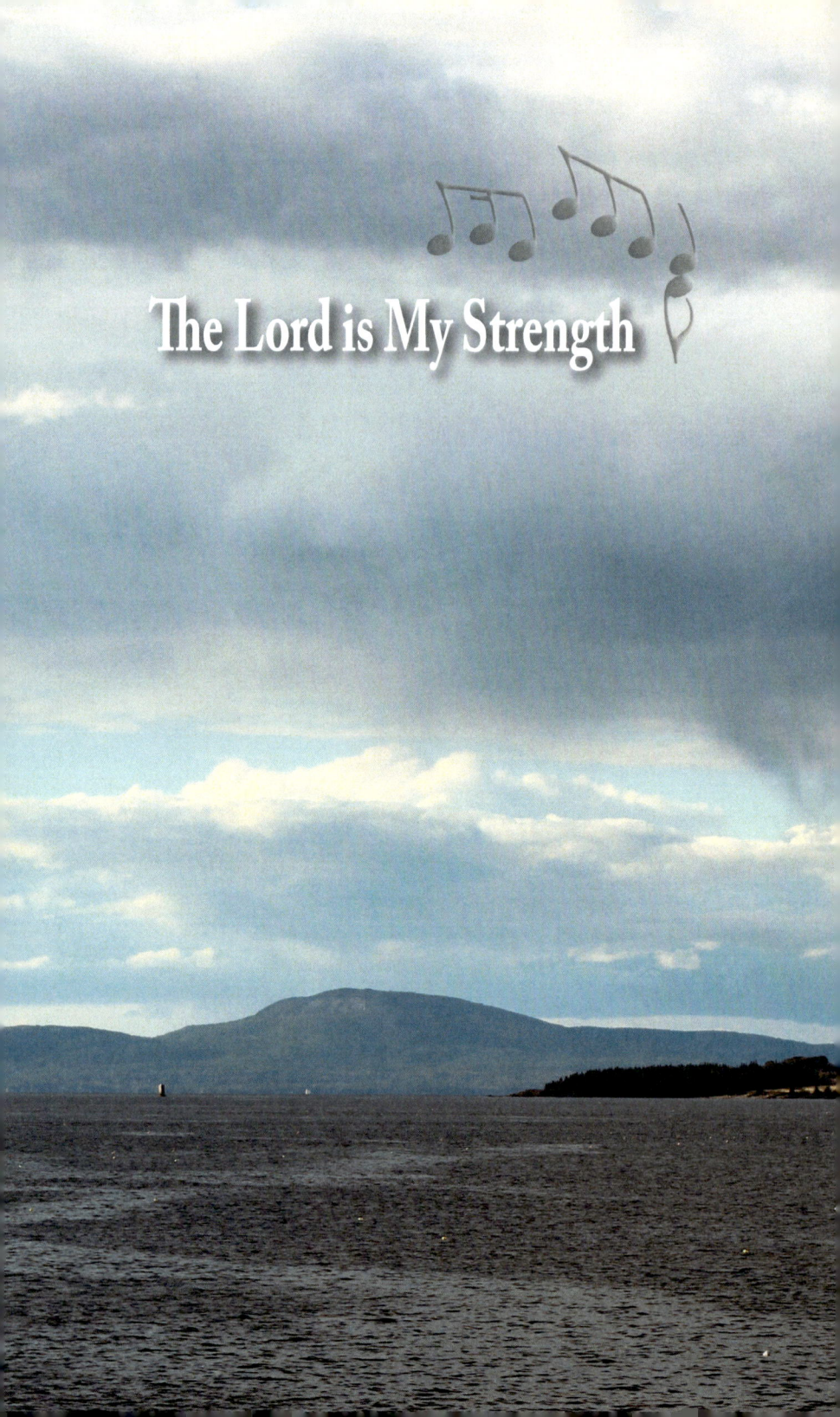

The Lord is My Strength

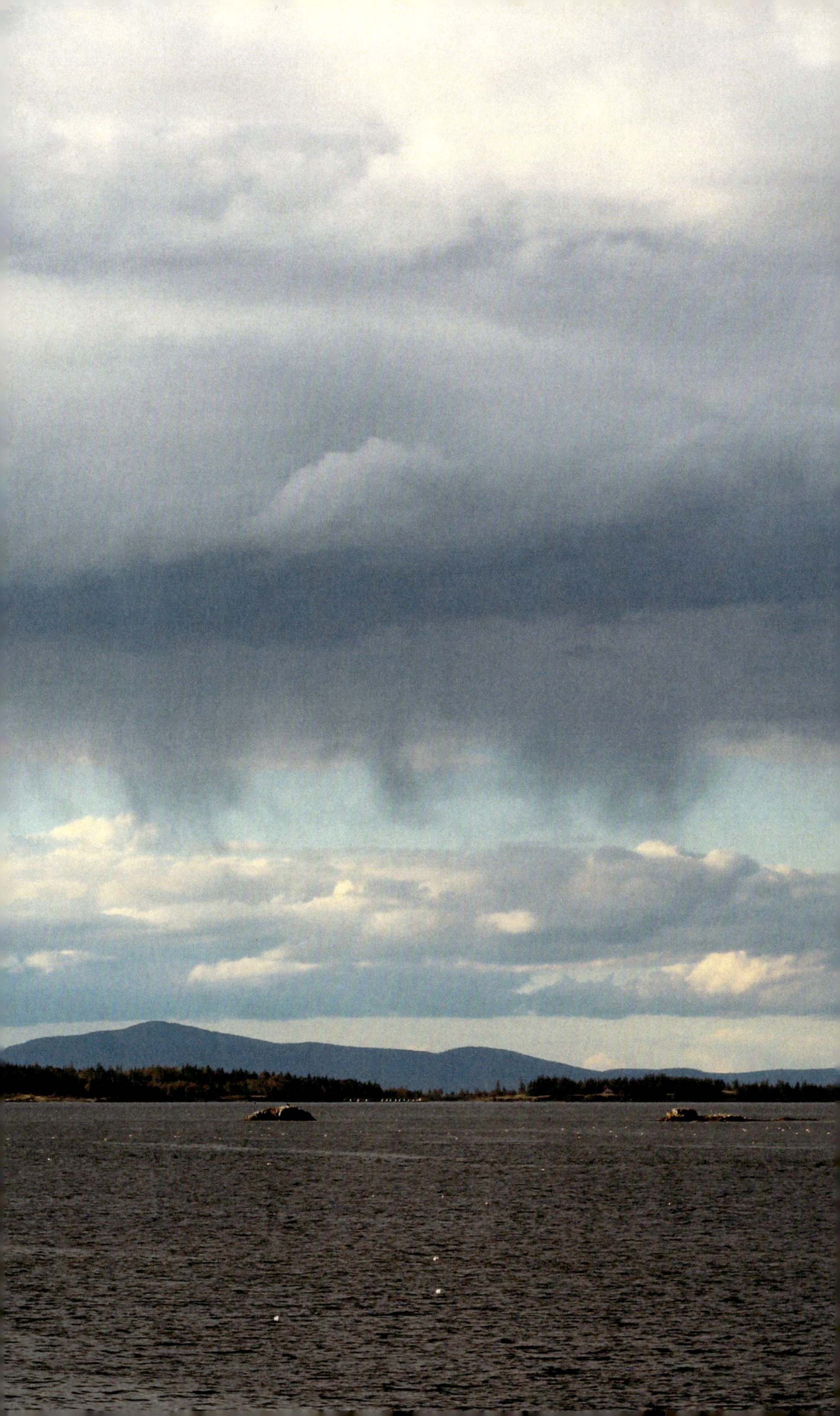

❦ STRENGTH ❦

The Lord is my strength;[1] I can do anything![2]
([1]Psalm 29:11. [2]Philippians 4:13.)

♪ Since my youth I have depended upon Him[3] to be my guide and counselor.[4] I stand fearless[5] and strong in Him.[6] *([3]1 John 2:14. [4]Psalm 73:24-26. [5]Psalm 27:1. [6]1 Corinthians 16:13.)*

♪ When I feel my weakness,[7] I call upon my Lord for help,[8] and He thunders through the Universe. The very foundation of wickedness is rebuked by the blast of His breath. He reaches out and draws me to Himself, protects me, gives me competence to meet the crisis, and empowers me to go forward.[9] In His strength I overcome temptation[10] and am made perfect. His gentleness has made me great.[9] *([7]2 Corinthians 12:9. [8]Psalm 105:4. [9]2 Samuel 22:5-17, 30-34. [10]1 Corinthians 10:13.)*

♪ Yet, I have fallen, and my strength has failed.[11] My weakness overwhelms me.[12] My heart is unsettled, my health is broken, my day has turned to darkness,[13] my friends turn away, and my adversaries plot mischief.[14] Yet, my

Lord is not far from me. I have hope. I will confess my sin[15] and wait. He shall renew my strength; I shall again fly like an eagle![16]
(*[11]Isaiah 40:29-31. [12]Psalm 31:10-12. [13]Psalm 38:3-10. [14]Psalm 21:11-13. [15]Psalm 38:15. [16]Psalm 103:5.*)

♪ It is time to celebrate for the joy of the Lord is my strength.[17] I shall give Him the glory due His name.[18] I will sing of His marvelous works.[19]
(*[17]Nehemiah 8:10. [18]Psalm 29:1, 2. [19]1 Chronicles 16:9-12.*)

♪ Surely the Lord is my strength, my song,[20] my salvation, and my God. I have prepared a habitation for Him in my heart, and He is preparing a place for me in heaven.[21] (*[20]Psalm 28:7. [21]Exodus 15:2, 13; John 14:1-3.*)

They that wait upon the Lord shall renew their strength. They shall mount up with wings as eagles; they shall run, and not be weary; and they shall walk, and not faint. ISAIAH 40:31

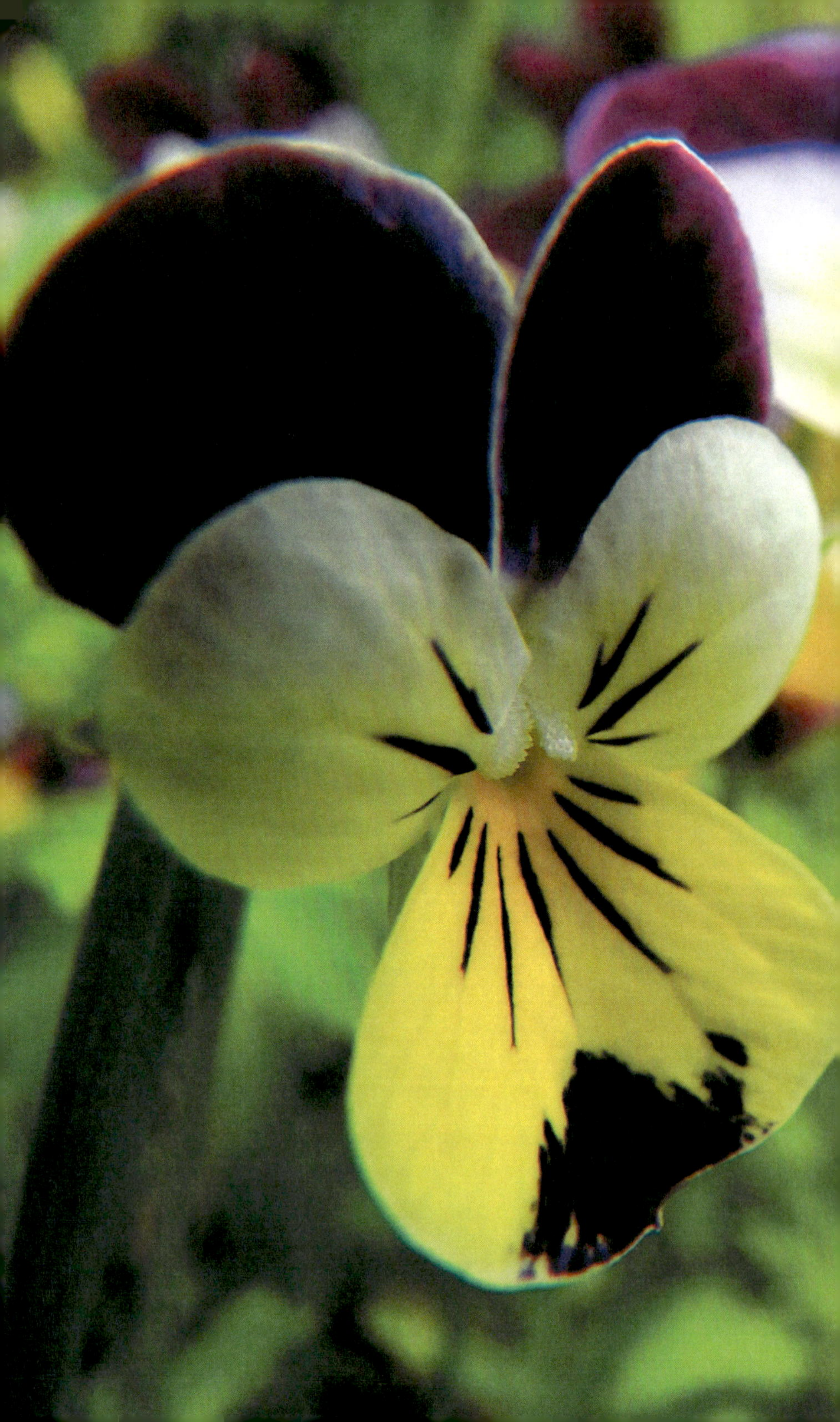

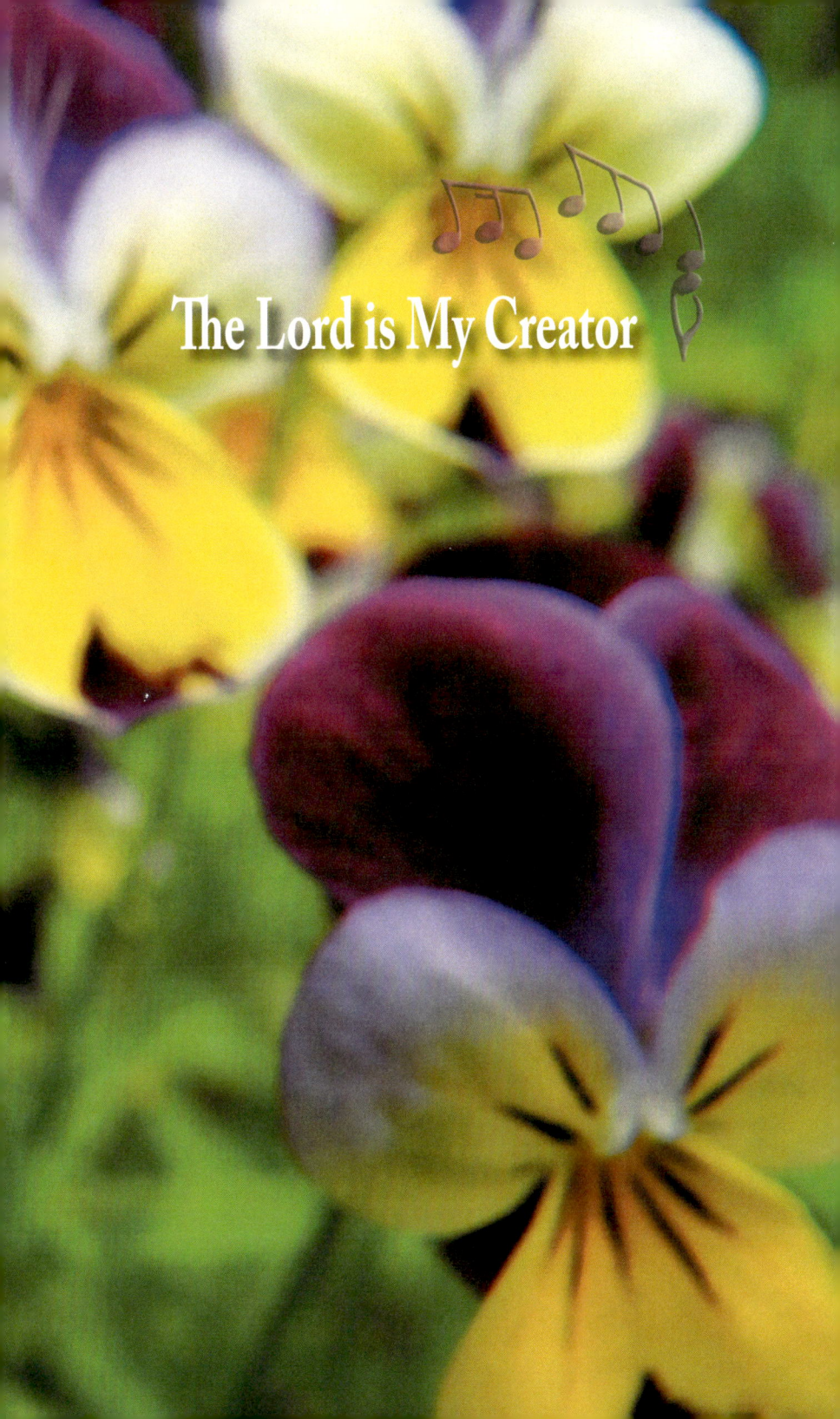

The Lord is My Creator

~ Creator ~

The Lord is my Creator;[1] I am but a speck of dust[2] in His great Universe.[3] *([1]Genesis 1:1. [2]Genesis 18:27. [3]Job 9:8-10; 38:31-33.)*

♪ When I consider the marvels of the heavens, the works of His fingers,[4] I am overwhelmed with my mortal[5] smallness[4] and His unsearchable[6] sinner-saving love![7] Just imagine, He made me a little lower than the angels[4] and trusted me with the grand responsibility of caring for my environment.[8] *([4]Psalm 8:3-6. [5]Genesis 3:19. [6]Psalm 145:3-12. [7]John 1:1-3, 14; John 3:16. [8]Isaiah 45:18. Genesis 1:26, 28.)*

♪ He laid the foundations of the earth[9] and stretched out the heavens with His hands. He poured forth light, and darkness followed.[10] He made the air, the water, the land, and every living plant and creature[11] by the word of His mouth.[12] He crowned His creation with mankind[13] and hallowed the Sabbath day for rest.[14] *([9]Job 38:4; Hebrews 1:10. [10]Isaiah 45:7, 12. [11]Genesis 1:1-27. [12]Psalm 33:6, 9. [13]Genesis 2:7, 8. [14]Genesis 2:1-3; Exodus 20:4-11.)*

♪ Who can be likened unto the Lord, the Creator? He is strong in power[15] and mighty in wisdom.[16] He sets a boundary for the sea and causes the bud to burst forth in the spring.[17] He controls the storehouse of the weather[18] and the movements of the heavenly bodies.[15] He made the animals with unique and marvelous abilities.[19] *([15]Isaiah 40:25-28. [16]Psalm 104:24. [17]Job 38:8, 11, 27. [18]Job 38:22-32. [19]Job chapters 39-40.)*

♪ It is all too wonderful for me![20] I will worship and bow down; I will kneel before the Lord my Maker.[21] Great and marvelous are His works![22] *([20]Job 42:3. [21]Psalm 95:3-7. [22]Revelation 15:3.)*

♪ Surely the everlasting God, the Creator[15] of the Universe,[23] is my God, and I shall worship Him[22] in the earth made new.[25] *([23]Colossians 1:16. [24]Isaiah 65:17.)*

By the word of the Lord were the heavens made; and all the host of them by the breath of His mouth.
PSALM 33:6

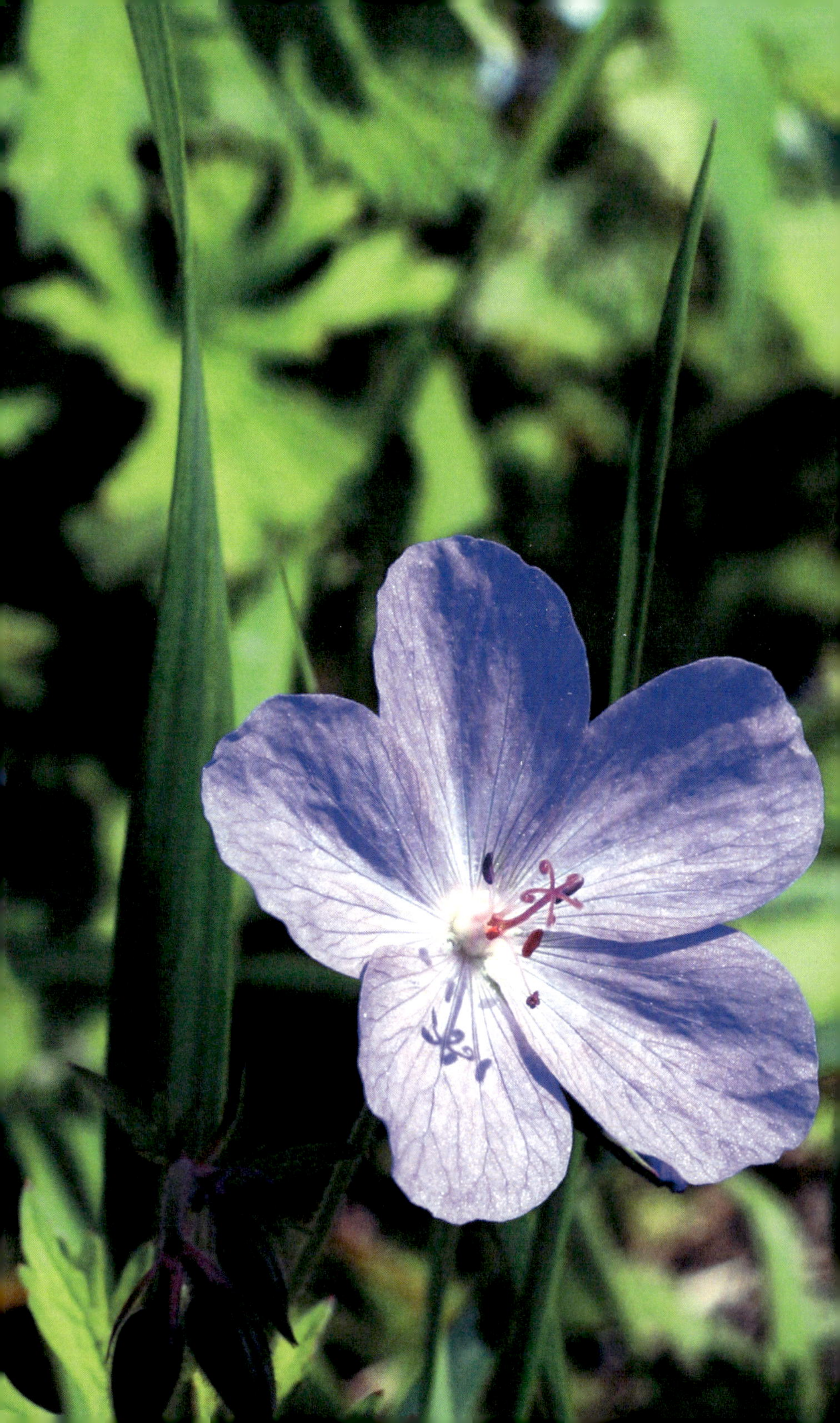

The Lord is My Comfort

COMFORT*

♪ The Lord is my comfort;[1] He shall wipe my tears away.[2] (*[1]1 Thessalonians 4:13, 14. [2]Revelation 21:4.*)

♪ He promises a day[3] when our dear, loving,[4] faithful[5] daughter and sister, who died without tasting death,[6] will live eternally[7] without any further burden[2] she felt for this wicked world. I rejoice that she is now at peace, for there is a life that is more bitter than death.[8] (*[3]Malachi 4:2. [4]1 John 3:14. [5]Revelation 2:10. [6]John 8:51, 52; Proverbs 12:28. [7]John 5:24. [8]Ecclesiastes 7:26 [reference here is to suffering being bitter, not snaring women]; Job 3:20-23.*)

♪ I am not in despair,[9] for I know her death is but a sleep before glory,[10] since Jesus, by whom she is forgiven,[11] through whom she learned obedience,[12] for whom she suffered,[13] in whom she placed her hope, and of whom she loved to speak[14] counts her righteous,[15] for He died in her place.[16] (*[9]1 Thessalonians 4:13-18. [10]Ecclesiastes 9:5; Psalm 13:3; John 11:13, 14. [11]1 John 2:1, 2. [12]Hebrews 5:7-9; 2 Timothy 1:9, 10. [13]Philippians 3:10. [14]1 Corinthians 2:1-4. [15]1 Corinthians 1:27-30. [16]Hebrews 2:9.*)

♪ God never forsook her. He was her constant help[17] and guide.[18] As they walked the valley together,[19] I cried out to her God, and He heard me.[20] He lifted me up from the gates of my daughter and sister's death and empowers me to, as He did her, show forth His praises and declare my assurance of her salvation.[21] *([17]Psalm 44:17-26. [18]Psalm 48:14. [19]Psalm 23:4. [20]Psalm 18:4-6. [21]Psalm 9:12-14.)*

♪ I cannot mourn without hope,[22] for I know that she gained the victory over death through her beloved Jesus.[23] Her death is gain, for the fruit of her labor lives on.[24] *([22]Proverbs 14:32; 1 Corinthians 15:55-57. [23]Psalm 116:12-19. [24]Philippians 1:20-21.)*

♪ Surely, I take up the cup of my salvation, offer a sacrifice of thanksgiving, and praise the Lord for I know that the death of our daughter and sister is precious in His sight.[23]

*Written in memory of 17 year old, Miriam Fleming, a precious child of God, whose passion for living and sharing God's love was an inspiration to all who knew her.

Precious in the sight of the Lord is the death of His saints. Psalm 116:15

The Lord is My Light, My Salvation,

and the Strength of My Life

~ LIFE* ~

The Lord is my light,[1] my salvation[2] and the strength[3] of my life, of whom shall I be afraid?[4] ([1]Luke 2:32. [2]Isaiah 12:2, 3. [3]Habakkuk 3:18, 19. [4]Jeremiah 42:11.)

♪ He trips up my adversaries.[5] In times of trouble He hides me under His wings,[6] sets me on a firm[7] rock,[8] and encamps His angels around about me.[6] When darkness surrounds me, He is my saving light.[9] ([5]Psalm 9:2, 3. [6]Psalm 91:4, 11. [7]Psalm 31:2. [8]Psalm 40:2. [9]Micah 7:8; Psalm 119:105; John 8:12.)

♪ In His sanctuary I find safety,[10] and in His strength I have enough confidence[11] to walk into the lion's den without fear.[12] ([10]Psalm 20:1, 2. [11]1 John 2:28; 29; Philippians 1:6; Proverbs 3:25, 26. [12]Daniel 6:22.)

♪ When I am forsaken,[13] He takes up my case.[14] He helps me,[15] teaches me,[16] leads me in a plain path[17] and protects me from harassment and false accusations.[18] He strengthens my heart and gives me courage.[19] *([13]Psalm 9:9, 10; 2 Corinthians 4:8, 9. [14]Hebrews 7:25. [15]Psalm 54:4; Isaiah 50:7-10. [16]Psalm 143:10; Psalm 86:11. [17]Psalm 5:8; Psalm 23:3. [18]Revelation 12:10; Psalm 40:13, 14. [19]Isaiah 40:31; Joshua 1:9.)*

♪ I wait on the Lord and seek to be with Him.[20] Oh, that I could dwell in His sanctuary all the days of my life. There I could look upon His beauty and ply Him with questions.[21] *([20]Psalm 37:34; Isaiah 8:17. [21]Exodus 25:8; Psalm 73:16, 17; Zechariah 13:6.)*

♪ Surely I have seen the goodness of the Lord. I will offer sacrifices of joy in His tabernacle. I will sing praises to His name.[22] *([22]Psalm 107:8-9; Psalm 116:12, 13, 17.)*

An expanded study of Psalm 27. Specific references to verses in Psalm 27 are not noted.

Teach me thy way, O Lord, and lead me in a plain path. **Psalm 27:11**

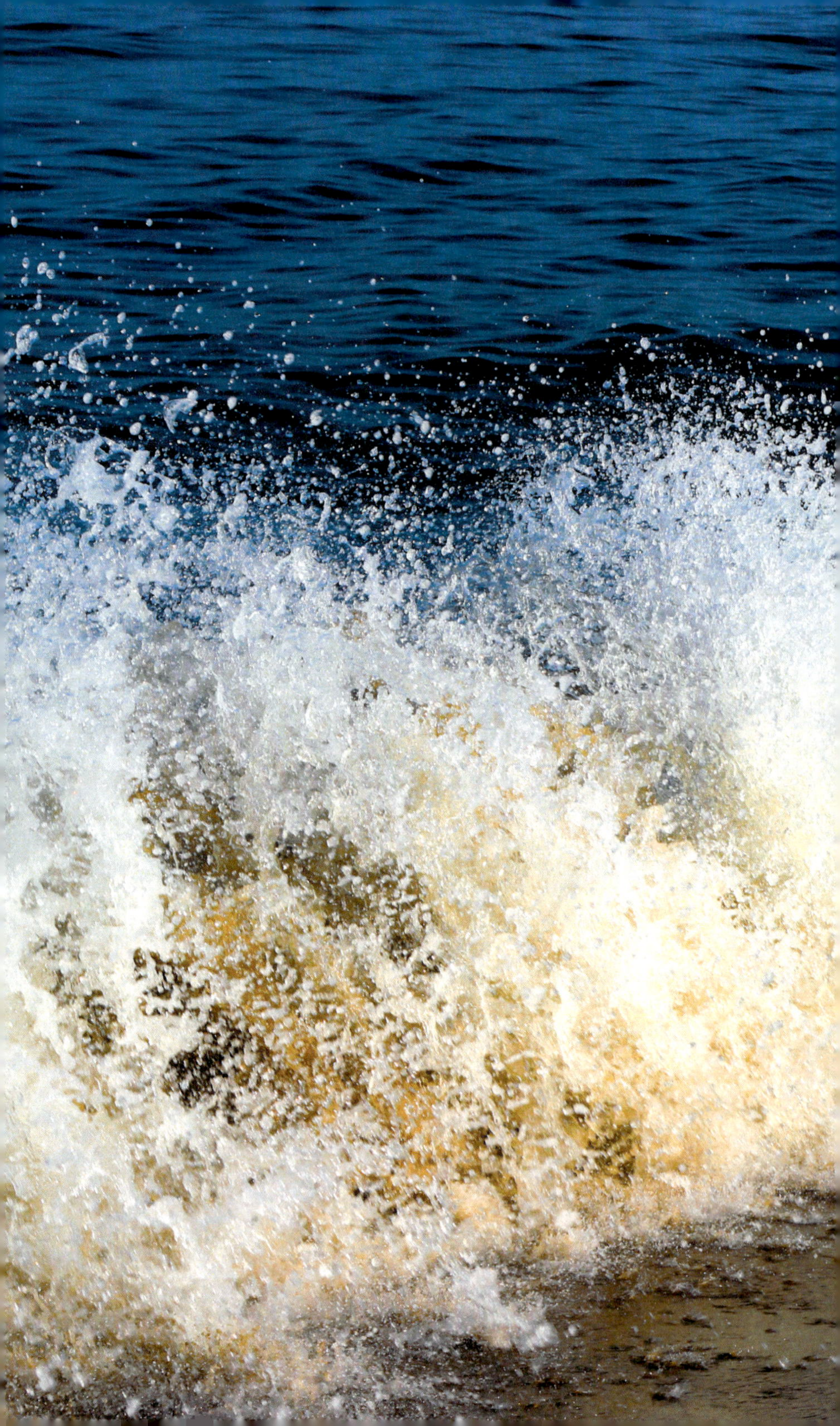

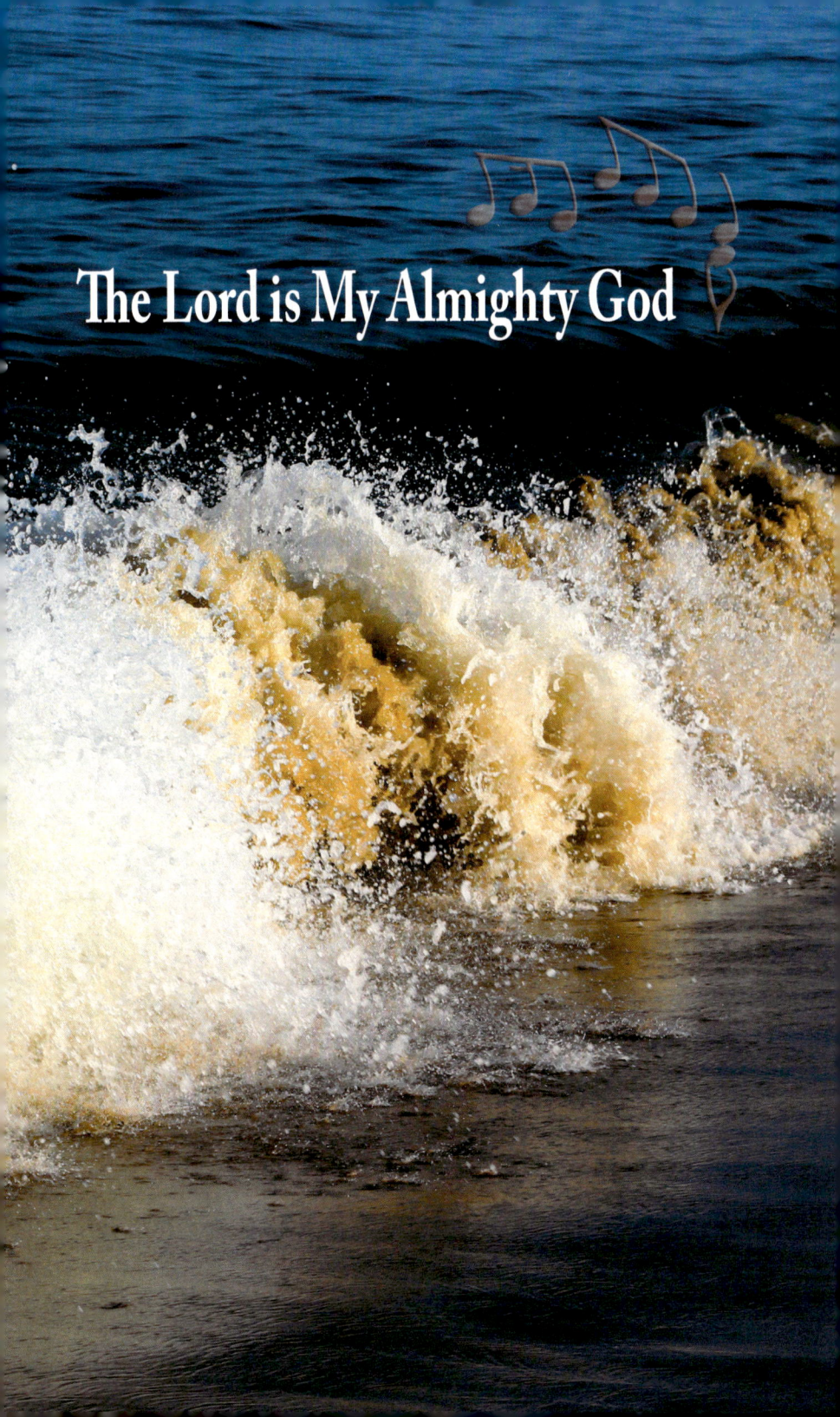

The Lord is My Almighty God

~ Almighty ~

The Lord is my almighty God;[1] I have set my love upon Him [2] and will walk before Him.[3] (*[1]Revelation 4:8, 11. [2]Psalm 91. [3]Genesis 17:1.*)

♪ I walk safely over rough places and past perilous situations in the day as well as in the night, for I abide under His shadow and am surrounded by His angels.[2]

♪ I once was blessed with prosperity and respected for my generosity, but right now I feel chastened.[4] (*[4]Job 29:2-17.*)

♪ He has dealt bitterly with me.[5] I am poisoned by His arrows and wish to die.[6] I do not understand,[7] yet I cling to the promise that He will hear my groaning and remove my burdens.[8] He says He will restore my honor.[9] I trust He will,[2] for His ways are just and true.[10] (*[5]Ruth 1:20. [6]Job 6:1-4, 9-17. [7]Job 11:7. [8]Exodus 6:3-6. [9]Ruth 4:11-17. [10]Revelation 15:2, 3.*)

♪ Soon I shall enter the Holy City,[11] and bow in thankful[12] worship to my Creator.[1] I will cry with the redeemed,[11] Holy, Holy, Holy

is the Lord God Almighty,
who is and was and is to come,[12] for He is
worthy to receive glory.[1] *([11]Matthew 25:34; Revelation 21:1-3, 22. [12]Revelation 4:8-11.)*

♪ Surely, I shall be satisfied with the life He gives me, for He has shown me His salvation.[2] Heaven is cheap enough![13]
([13]Revelation 2:10; 21:1-23.)

Behold, happy is the man whom God correcteth: therefore despise not thou the chastening of the Almighty. JOB 5:17

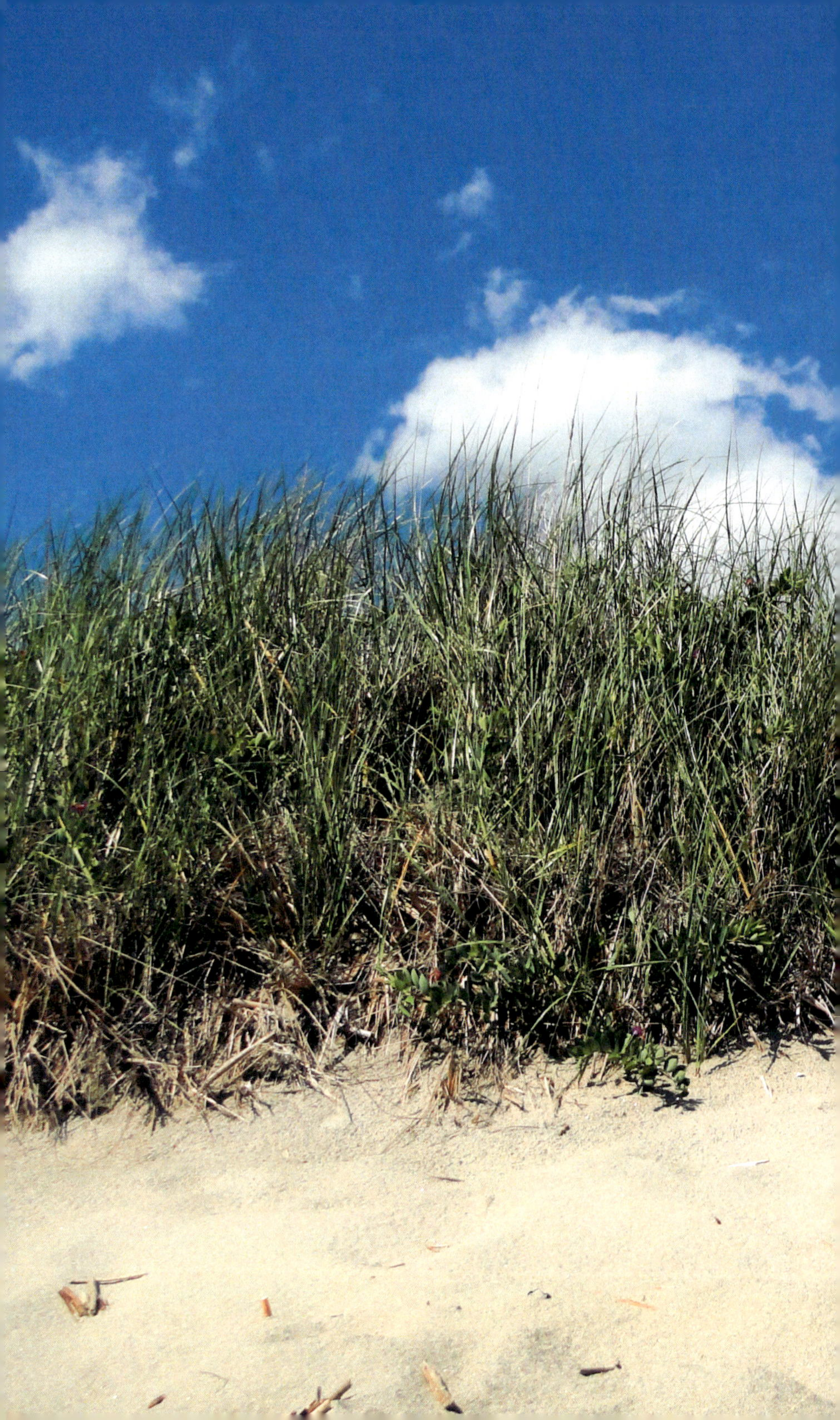

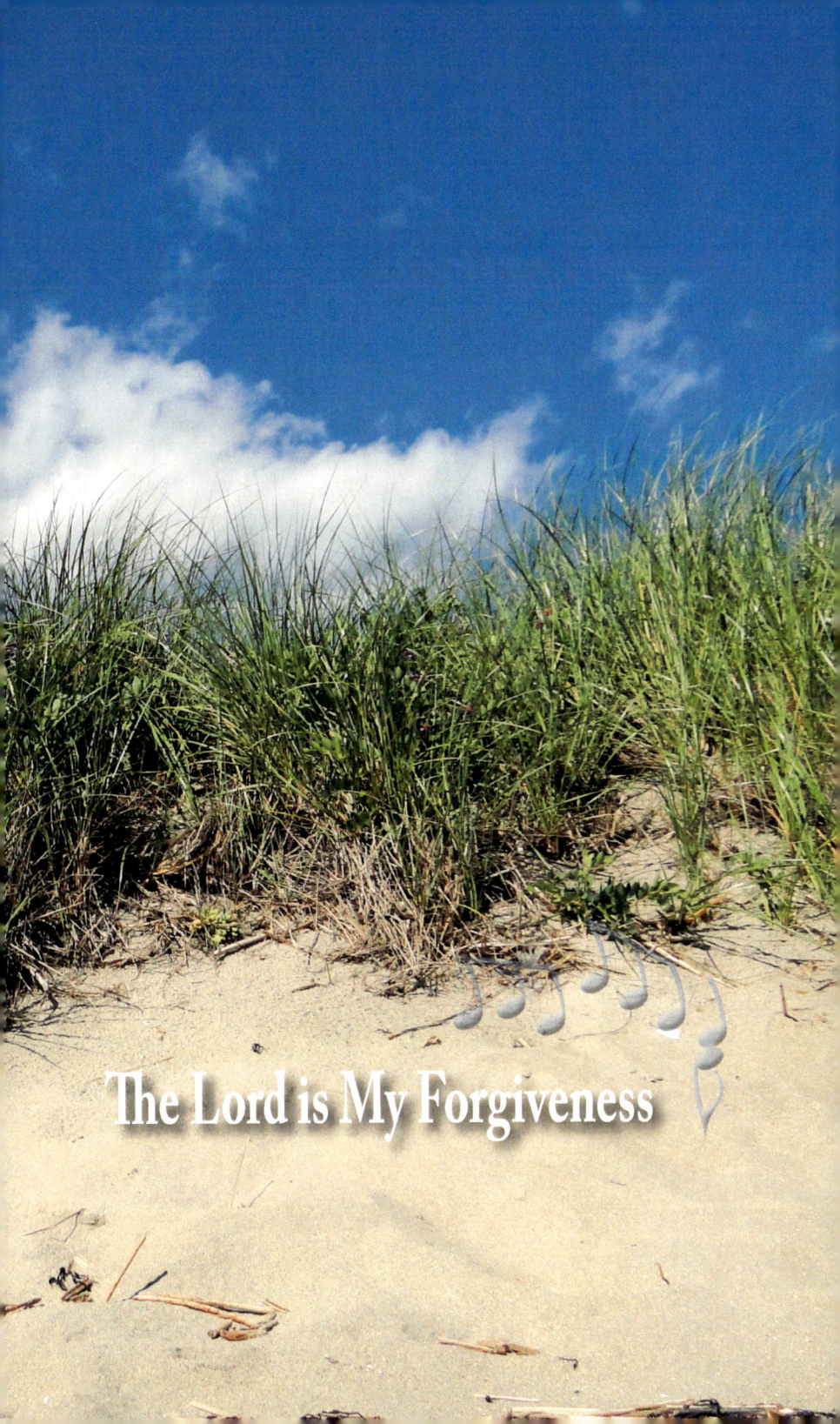

The Lord is My Forgiveness

~ WORDS ~

The Lord is my forgiveness; I blew it again, but when I called upon Him, He extended His mercy.[1] *([1]Psalm 86:5, 6. Psalm 89:1.)*

♪ What can I say? I tried to speak comforting words to a weary soul,[2] but my good words were tainted with evil,[3] my tongue betrayed my inner feelings,[4] my words cut to the core,[5] and instead of healing and comforting, they wounded.[6] *([2]Isaiah 50:4. [3]James 3:5-10. [4]Proverbs 4:23, 24. [5]Psalm 52:2. [6]Proverbs 12:18.)*

♪ I am captive to my own selfish thoughts.[7] I am constantly saying what I don't want to say.[8] I speak of my Lord's righteousness and use the tongue He gave me to praise His name,[9] yet my words often prove that I am double minded and proud.[10] *([7]2 Corinthians 10:5. [8]Romans 7:15. [9]Psalm 35:28. [10]Psalm 12:3, 4.)*

♪ I need Him to cleanse me and give me right attitudes,[11] acceptable thoughts and pure words.[12] I need Him to bridle my lips, take away my voice, and silence me,[13] for I desire to speak no guile,[14] no bitter words,[15] no unloving rebukes, and no flattering pleasantries.[16] *([11]Isaiah 6:5-7. [12]Psalm 19:14. [13]Psalm 39:1-3. [14]Psalm 34:11-15. [15]Psalm 64:3. [16]Proverbs 28:23.)*

♪ I cry to Him and instead of condemning me,[17] He forgives me,[18] washes me clean,[19] fills me with His Spirit,[20] changes my heart,[21] brings my thoughts into obedience to His will,[22] and leads me into victory.[23] *([17]Romans 8:1. [18]1 John 1:9. [19]Psalm 51:2-10. [20]Psalm 139:23, 24. [21]Ezekiel 36:26, 27. [22]2 Corinthians 10:5; Philippians 1:6. [23]Romans 8:37.)*

♪ Surely my mouth is filled with laughter and my tongue with singing, for my captivity is turned. The Lord has done great things for me, and I am glad.[24] *([24]Psalm 126:1, 2.)*

Let the words of my mouth and the meditations of my heart be acceptable in thy sight. PSALM 19:14

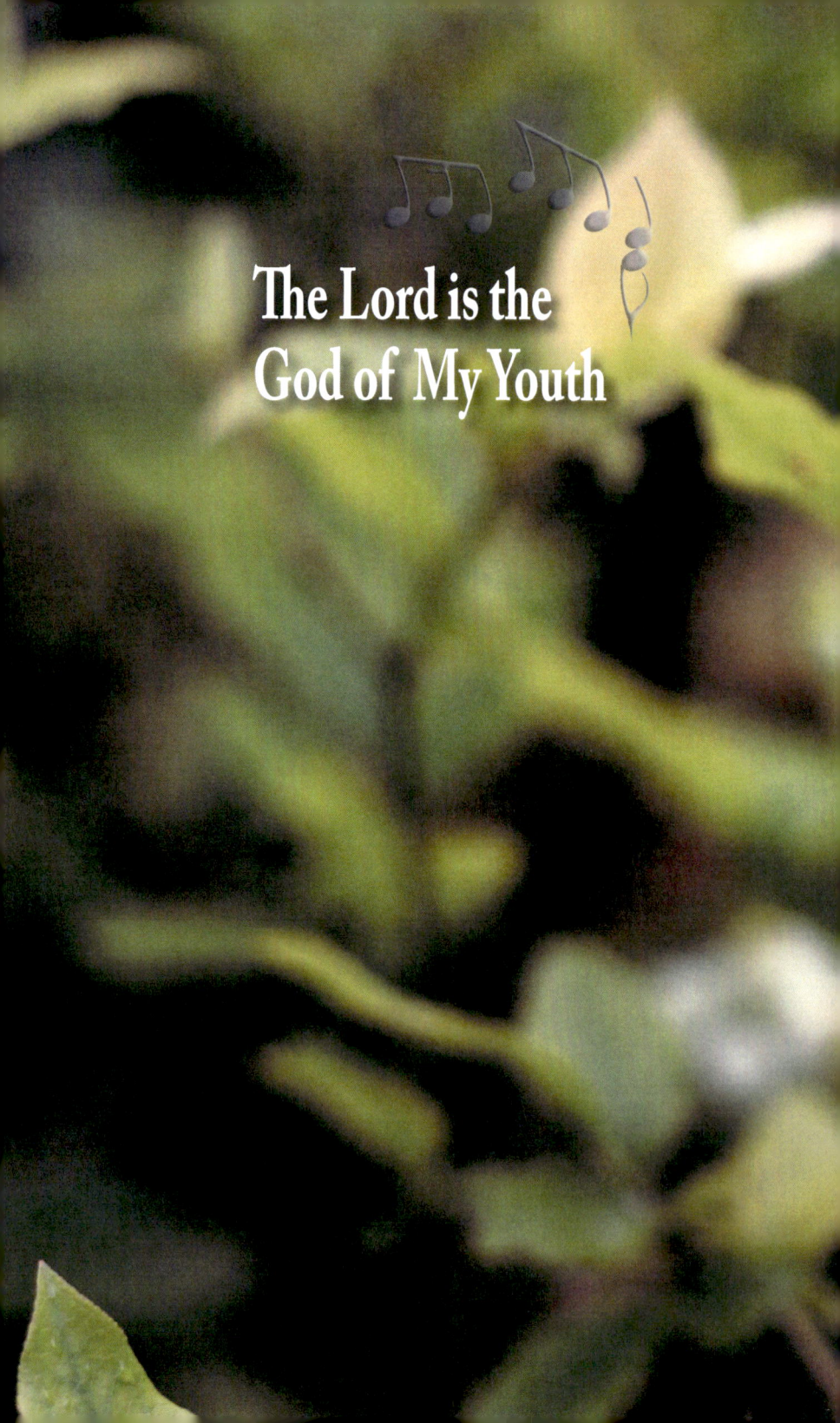

The Lord is the
God of My Youth

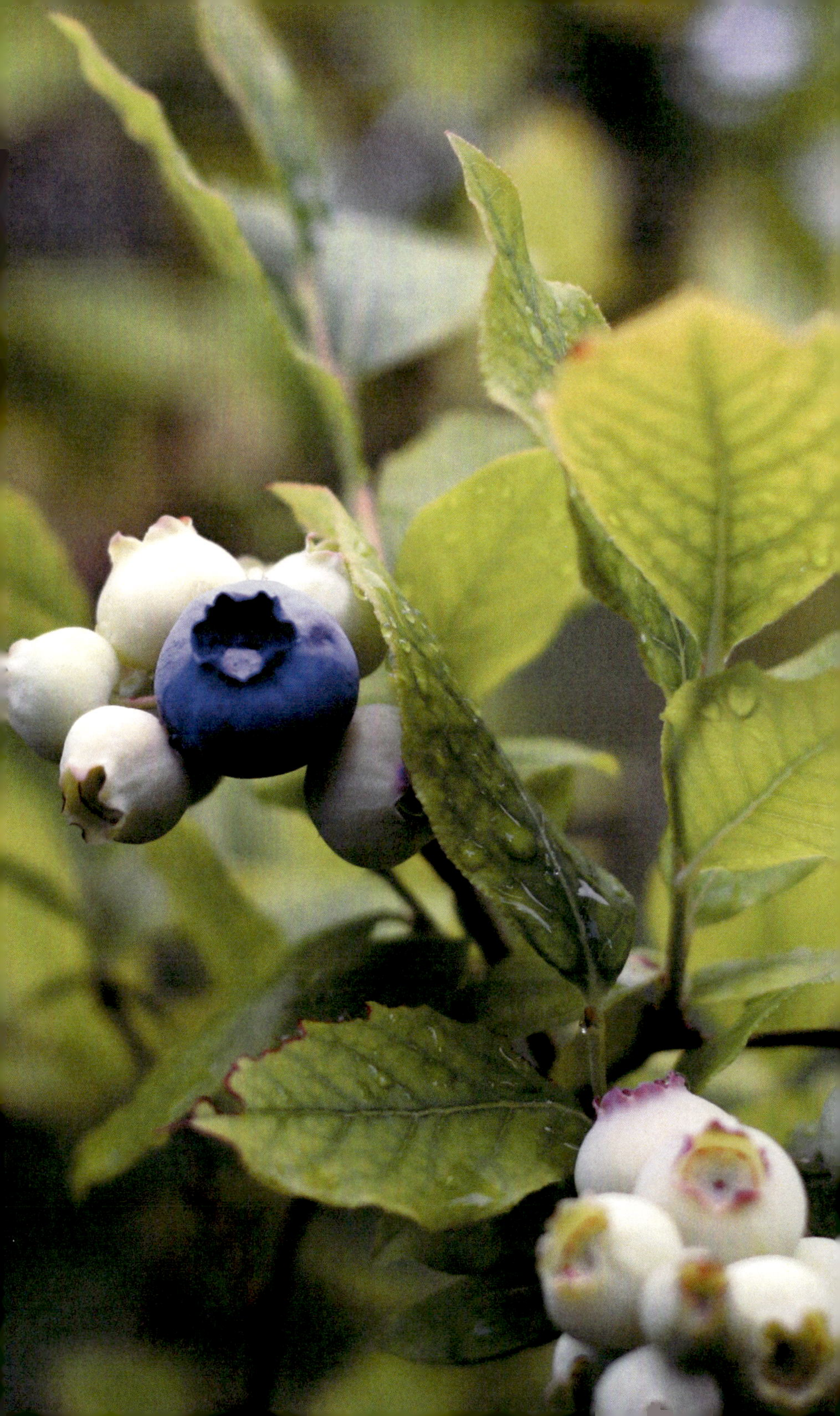

~ YOUTH ~

The Lord is the God of my youth; I shall trust[1] His guidance.[2] *([1]Psalm 71:5, 17. [2]Jeremiah 3:4.)*

♪ Through following His counsel I am empowered to choose good[3] and avoid future bitterness.[4] He looks past my youthful foolishness and patiently teaches me a better way.[5] *([3]Psalm 103:5-7. [4]Proverbs 5:1-4. [5]Psalm 25:7-13.)*

♪ The Lord is my Creator! This knowledge gives me inner joy and a zest for life.[6] I can face the trials and temptations of the future as they come, for the Lord is my God.[7] I can rise above the "they-are but-youth" mind-set and be an example of a faith-filled, pure life.[8] *([6]Ecclesiastes 11:9-12:1. [7]Psalm 144:12-15. [8]1 Timothy 4:12.)*

♪ Though I fall into sin,[9] though my inexperienced, willful imagination turns to evil,[10] and though I trust my own accomplishment,[11] I am not forsaken. In His wisdom and everlasting kindness,[12] He allows

trials[11] and consequences to be my teacher.[13]
([9]Isaiah 40:30. [10]Genesis 8:21. [11]Jeremiah 48:11.
[12]Isaiah 54:6-7. [13]Psalm 88:14-15.)

♪ I know He will bring good upon me, just as He promised.[14] This gives me hope. I will trustingly wait.[15] ([14]Jeremiah 32:36-42. [15]Lamentations 3:25-33.)

♪ Surely, while I can still enjoy life, I will seek the pleasures[6] of my sanctified heart, and I, with my children, shall inherit the earth.[15]

For Thou art my hope, O Lord God: Thou art my trust from my youth. PSALM 71:5

∽ 73 ∾

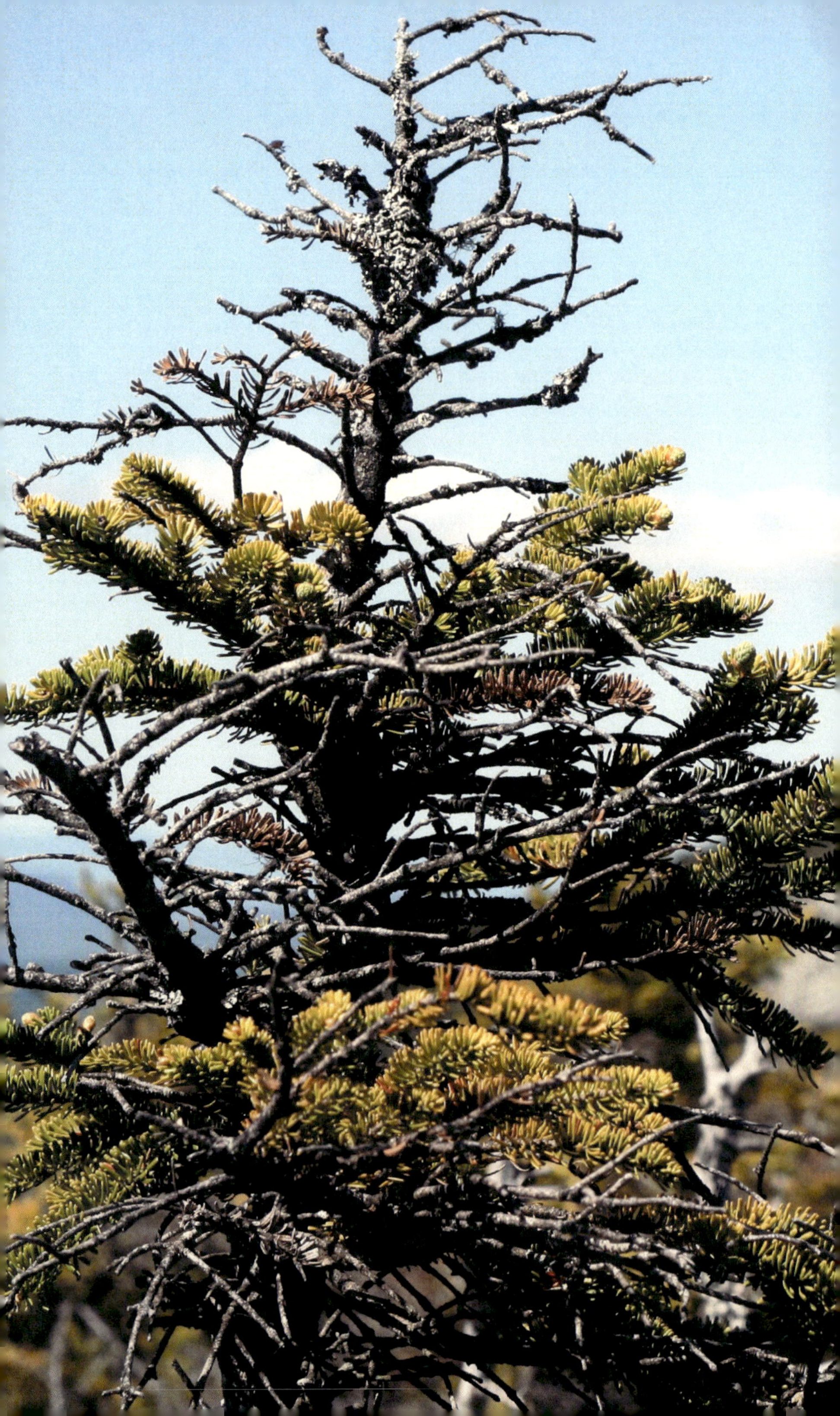

The Lord is the God of My Old Age

~ Old Age* ~

The Lord is the God of my old age; I shall trust Him until the day I turn to dust.[1] *([1]Job 13:15.)*

♪ I will speak of His righteousness[2] and praise Him continually,[3] for I know not the number of my days.[4] *([2]Psalm 35:28. [3]Hebrews 13:13-16. [4]Psalm 90:10-12.)*

♪ I am old and grey headed. My strength fails. I am easily confused; my eyes are dim; my tears are dried up; my teeth are few; I walk with a cane; I am startled by the song of a bird but cannot discern the voice of a man. Life has lost its zest. My only hope is in the Lord.[5] *([5]2 Peter 3:13.)*

♪ I have become the target of unrighteous and unscrupulous men. They plan to take advantage of me. They think I am forsaken, but I am not! Although my health is broken and my life is ebbing,[6] I go forward in His strength. He has blessed me from my youth.[7] He will not forsake me now![8] *([6]2 Corinthians 4:16-18. [7]Isaiah 40:29-31. [8]Psalm 37:25.)*

~ 76 ~

♪ I shall soon turn to dust, for I am nearing the end of my course, and my departure is at hand.[9] Though I am failing in strength, I have gladness in my heart and can sleep in peace[10] for I am not afraid to die.[11] *([9]2 Timothy 4:6-9. [10]Psalm 4:7, 8. [11]2 Corinthians 5:1, 2; Psalm 23:4.)*

♪ Surely the day will come when I shall walk on streets of gold without any pain[12] for Lord will raise me up from the depths of the earth, take me to His home, and place a crown of righteousness upon my head.[9] Then will I sing His praises and speak of His goodness forever. *([12]Revelation 21:4, 21.)*

*Written in the wake of our dear friend Eddie McWilliams' passing. An expanded study of aging from Psalm 71 and Ecclesiastes 12. Specific verses from these chapters are not noted.

In thee, O Lord, do I put my trust: let me never be put to confusion. **Psalm 71:1**

The Lord is My Rock

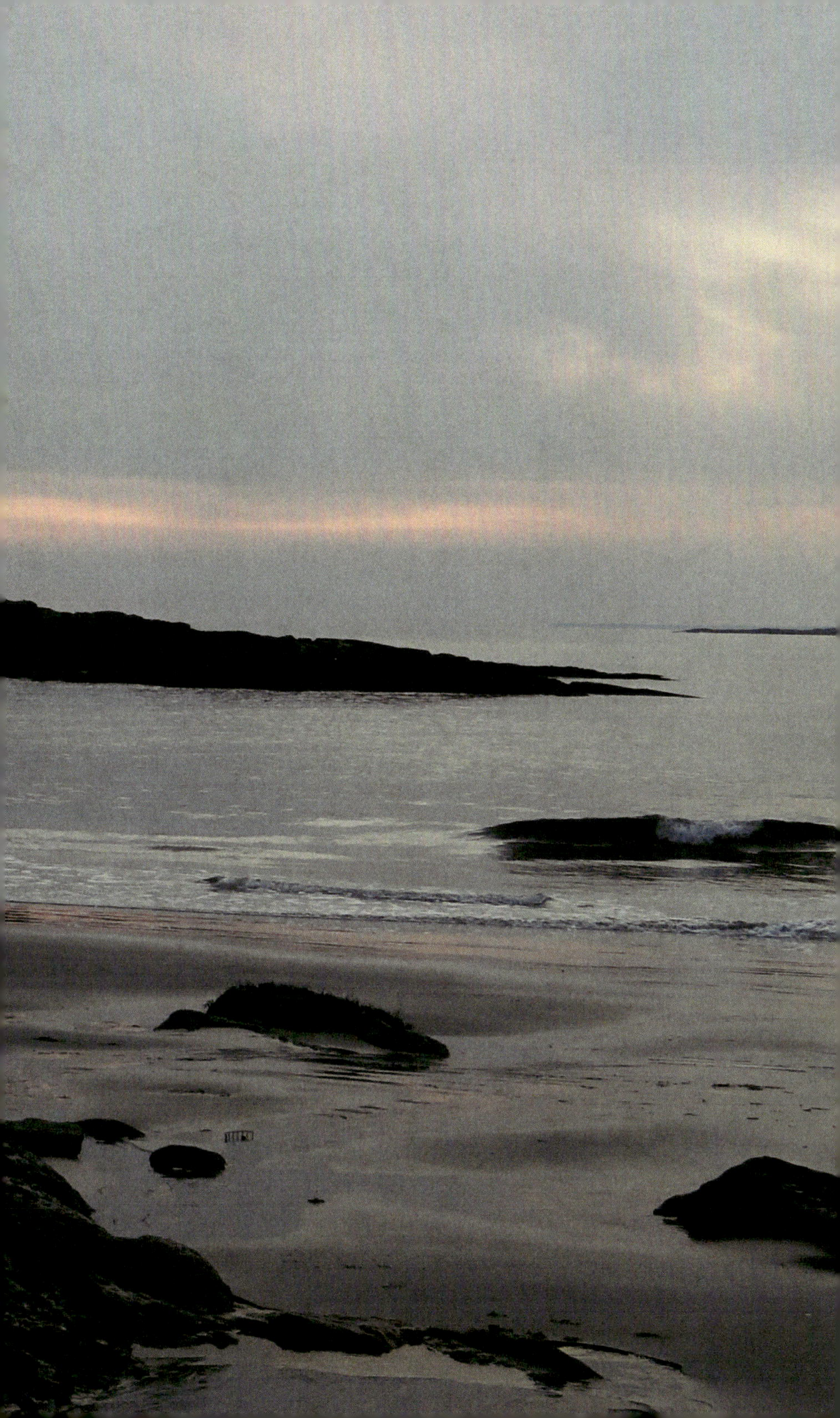

~ Rock ~

The Lord is my rock of salvation; I shall not be moved.[1] *([1]Psalm 62:1, 2.)*

♪ He feeds me with fine wheat and honey out of the Rock.[2] Living[3] water gushes forth[4] and my thirst is quenched.[3] *([2]Psalm 81:16. [3]John 4:10-13. [4]Isaiah 48:21.)*

♪ He sets my feet upon the rock and establishes my goings.[5] For His name sake, He not only leads me[6] in the perfect way, but gives me strength and power to follow.[7] *([5]Psalm 27:5; Psalms 40:2. [6]Psalm 31:3. [7]2 Samuel 22:33; Psalms 18:32.)*

♪ The Lord is my Rock, my Fortress, my Deliverer, my Shield, my Horn of Salvation, my High Tower, and my Refuge. He is my Savior. In Him will I trust.[8] *([8]2 Samuel 22:3; Psalm 18:2.)*

♪ Oh, my God, when I am overwhelmed: lead me to the Rock that is higher than I.[9] Let the Rock of my salvation be exalted.[10] *([9]Psalm 61:1, 2. [10]Psalm 18:46; 2 Samuel 22:47.)*

♪ Surely my salvation is solid, my faith shall not waiver,[11] and I will walk on streets of gold forever.[12] *([11]Isaiah 28:16. [12]Revelation 21:21.)*

O come, let us sing unto the Lord: let us make a joyful noise to the Rock of our salvation. **Psalm 95:1**

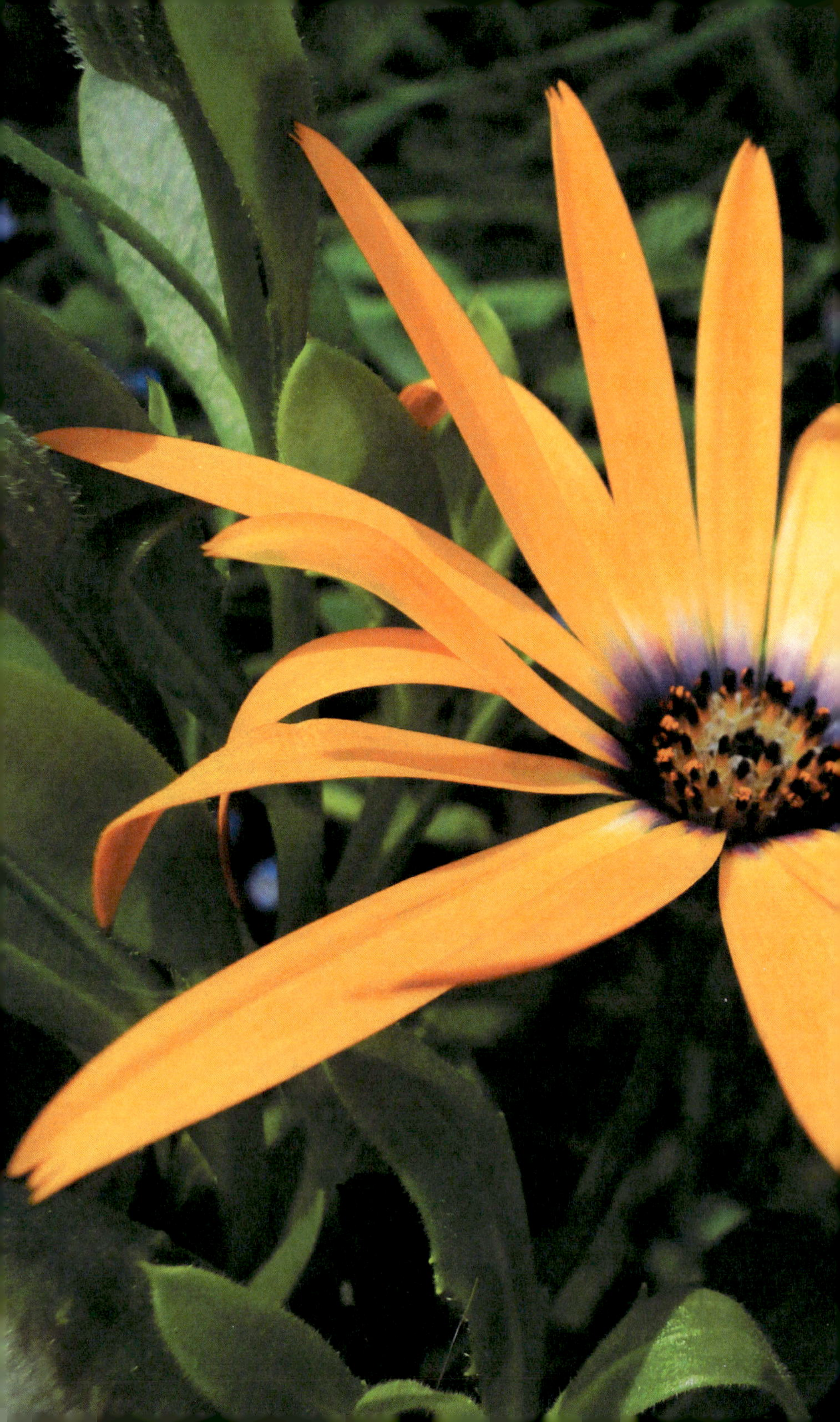

The Lord is My Counselor

~ Counselor ~

The Lord is my wonderful counselor;[1] I shall seek Him early.[2] (*[1]Isaiah 9:6. [2]Proverbs 8:14, 17.*)

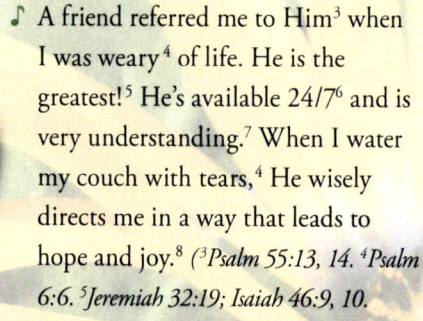

♪ A friend referred me to Him[3] when I was weary[4] of life. He is the greatest![5] He's available 24/7[6] and is very understanding.[7] When I water my couch with tears,[4] He wisely directs me in a way that leads to hope and joy.[8] (*[3]Psalm 55:13, 14. [4]Psalm 6:6. [5]Jeremiah 32:19; Isaiah 46:9, 10. [6]Psalm 16:7. [7]Job 12:13. [8]Psalm 16:8-11.*)

♪ The counsel of the unrighteous[9] leads to despair,[10] but when I heed the Lord's counsels and turn from my evil ways,[11] my heart is strengthened,[12] and I find the way of salvation.[13] (*[9]Psalm 1:1. [10]Isaiah 30:1; Psalm 107:11-21. [11]Jeremiah 23:21, 22. [12]Psalm 73:24-28. [13]Psalm 20:4-6.*)

♪ I trust only my Lord who, after all, is the Father of counseling.[14] His solutions are designed to meet my specific needs[15] and renew my strength.[16] *([14]Job chapters 38-41; Isaiah 40:13, 14; Romans 11:33-36. [15]Psalm 33:10-15; Jeremiah 32:19. [16]Isaiah 40:31.)*

♪ When I follow His counsels, my eyes are opened, and I see that my fiery trials are actually refining me.[17] *([17]Revelation 3:18.)*

♪ Surely my days are lengthened,[18] yet I face death with hope, for I know He will, when He comes,[19] receive me into glory[12] where there shall be peace forevermore.[20] *([18]Job 12:12. [19]Psalm 16:8-11; Ephesians 1:10-14. [20]Isaiah 9:7.)*

Thou shalt guide me with thy counsel, and afterward receive me into glory. **Psalm 73:24**

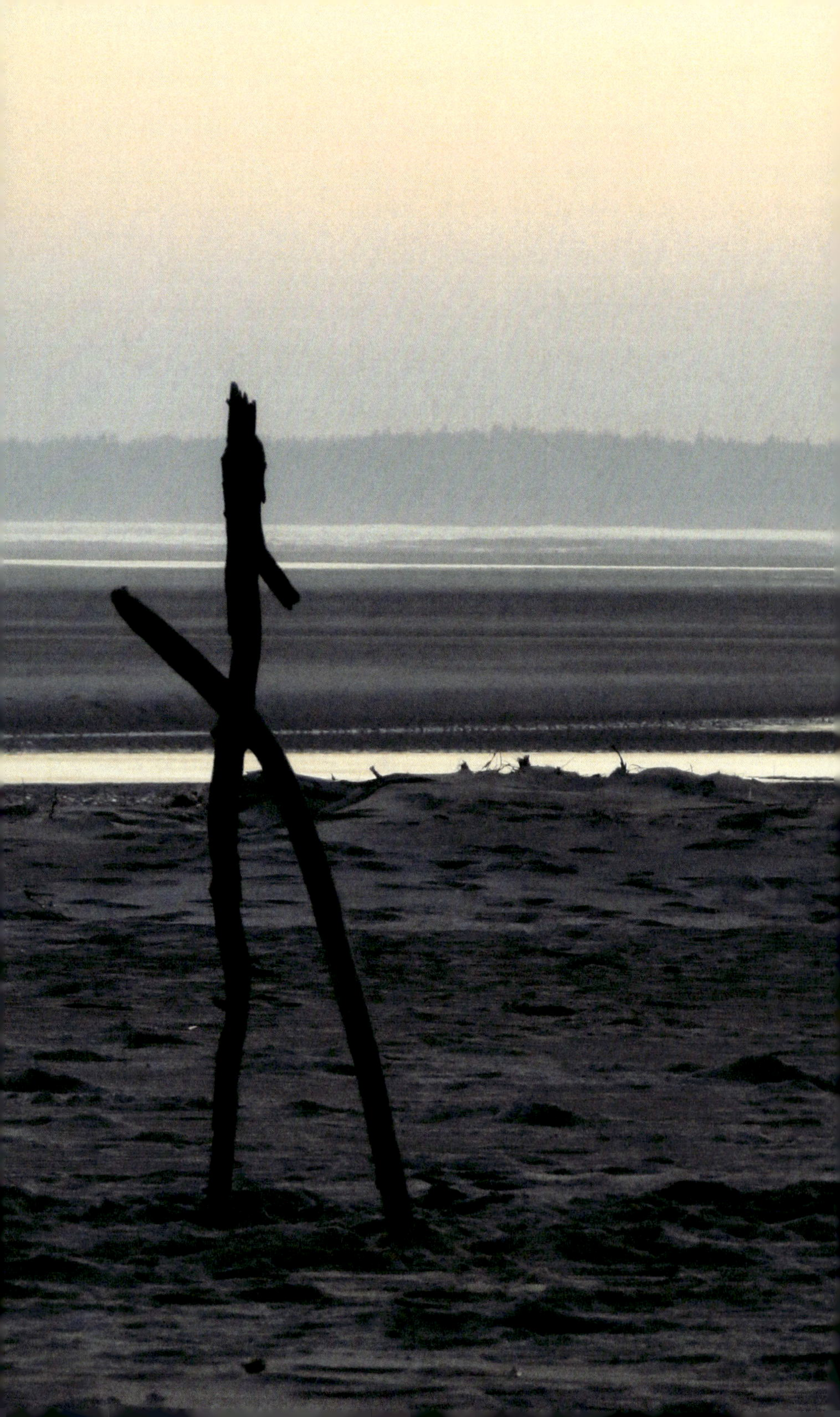

The Lord is
My Sovereign God

TRAGEDY[*]

The Lord is my sovereign God; in Him will I trust[1]—even if He slays me,[2] or my children.[3] *([1]Psalm 91:2. [2]Job 13:15. [3]Job 1:18-22.)*

♪ He promises to lead me and provide for me,[4] yet I am afflicted and feel forsaken.[5] I know He has good plans for my life,[6] yet my soul is full of troubles.[7] My tears are my meat day and night.[8] In my distress[9] I cry out, where are you? Why have you forgotten me?[7] He replies, "Give me time; you will see."[10] *([4]Psalm 23:1, 2. [5]Isaiah 49:8-14. [6]Jeremiah 29:11. [7]Psalm 42:9-11. [8]Psalm 88:3-9. [9]Psalm 18:6. [10]Isaiah 54:11.)*

♪ He disciplines me in love,[11] and teaches me obedience[12] and patience through trial.[13] Though I groan[14] under this refining process,[15] I shall yet praise the Lord my God![7] *([11]Hebrews 12:6. [12]Psalm 119:67, 71. [13]James 1:3, 4; James 5:10-11; 1 Peter 1:7, 8. [14]Psalm 102:1-5. [15]Zechariah 13:9.)*

♪ He has compassion upon me,[16] lifts me up when my foot slips,[17] and comforts me with the promise that He will, in His time,[18] restore what has been taken.[19] I will quietly wait.[20] ([16]Lamentations 3:32-33. [17]Psalm 37:23, Psalm 91:11-12. [18]Ecclesiastes 3:10, 11. [19]Joel 2:25. [20]Lamentations 3:24-26; Micah 7:7.)

♪ The Lord is my God, whom, though I have not seen, I love.[21] He has engraven me and my children upon the palms of His hands.[22] I know He will deliver me,[23] and establish my goings.[24]
([21]1 John 4:12. [22]Isaiah 49:16. [23]Psalm 91:14, 15. [24]Psalm 40:2.)

♪ Surely my latter end shall be more blessed than the first,[25] for I, with my children,[26] shall see His face.[27] ([25]Job 42:12. [26]Isaiah 49:17-25. [27]Job 19:26.)

*Written following the December 14, 2012, Sandy Hook Elementary School shooting

Though He slay me, yet will I trust in Him. JOB 13:15

The Lord is My Light

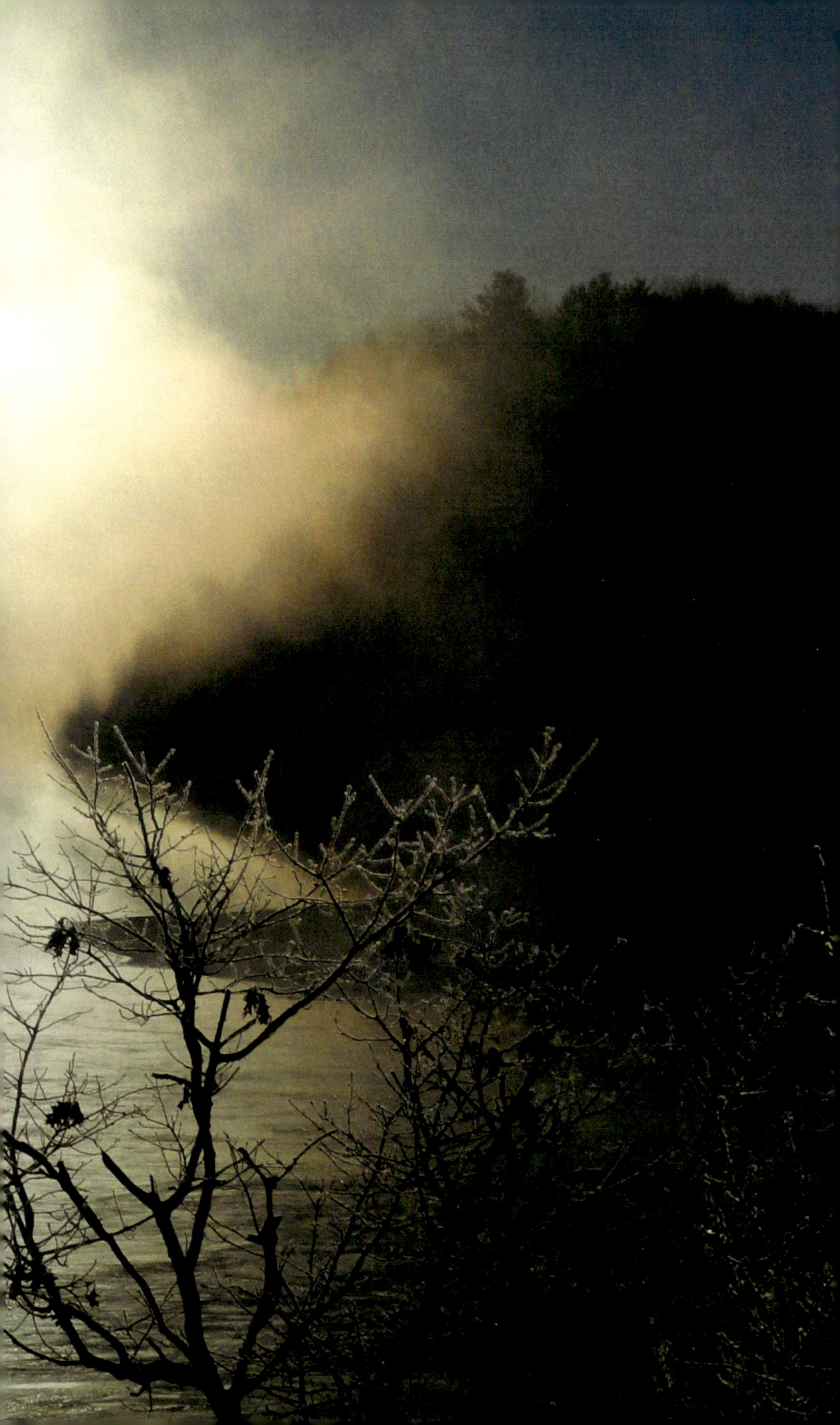

~ LIGHT ~

♪ *The Lord* is my light;[1] I no longer stumble in darkness,[2] for I have been called to walk[3] in the light shining from His face.[4] *([1]John 1:9. [2]John 11:9 10; Isaiah 59:9-10. [3]1 Peter 2:9. [4]2 Corinthians 4:6.)*

♪ As we walk[5] and talk[6] together, I turn from my weapons of self-defense[7] and trust Him for protection.[8] His light dispels the darkness from my heart[9] and helps me exchange my heavy burden for His "light" one.[10] *([5]Psalm 89:15. [6]1 John 1:7. [7]Isaiah 2:4, 5. [8]Psalm 89:18. [9]John 3:19-21. [10]Matthew 11:30.)*

♪ He becomes my armor of light[11] and gives me confidence,[12] as I fight the battle for my soul.[13] His light exposes lustful entertainment, riotous living,[13] and careless indolence, for the shameful, unfruitful foolishness[14] that they really are.[15] *([11]Romans 13:12-14. [12]Psalm 27:1-3. [13]1 Peter 2:9-11. [14]Ephesians 5:8-17. [15]John 12:35, 36.)*

♪ His light dispels the depressing darkness of trouble, perplexity, persecution, and discouragement.[16] It gives me clear vision,[17] shows me His will, sheds light upon the future,[18] guides my feet in the way of peace,[19] and leads me to seek forgiveness.[20] *([16]2 Corinthians 4:8-9. [17]John 9:4-7; Acts 26:18. [18]2 Peter 1:19; 1 Thessalonians 5:4; Daniel 2:22. [19]Luke 1:79. [20]Acts 26:18)*

♪ The Lord is my Light and my salvation. Oh, that I would ever walk in that light and reflect it in how I treat[21] others[22] that they too would find the way to salvation[23] and, with me, glorify His name.[24] *([21]Isaiah 58:6-10. [22]Acts 13:47. [23]Isaiah 49:5, 6. [24]Matthew 5:14-16.)*

♪ Surely my joy is full[25] and I, and those with whom I have shared[26] the everlasting Light,[27] shall be given an inheritance in my Lord's kingdom,[28] where there is no darkness,[29] for He is the light.[30] *([25]1 John 1:4. [26]Acts 26:18. [27]Isaiah 60:20. [28]Colossians 1:12, 13. [29]Revelation 22:5. [30]Revelation 21:23, 24.)*

When I sit in darkness, the Lord shall be a light unto me. Micah 7:8

The Lord is My Refuge

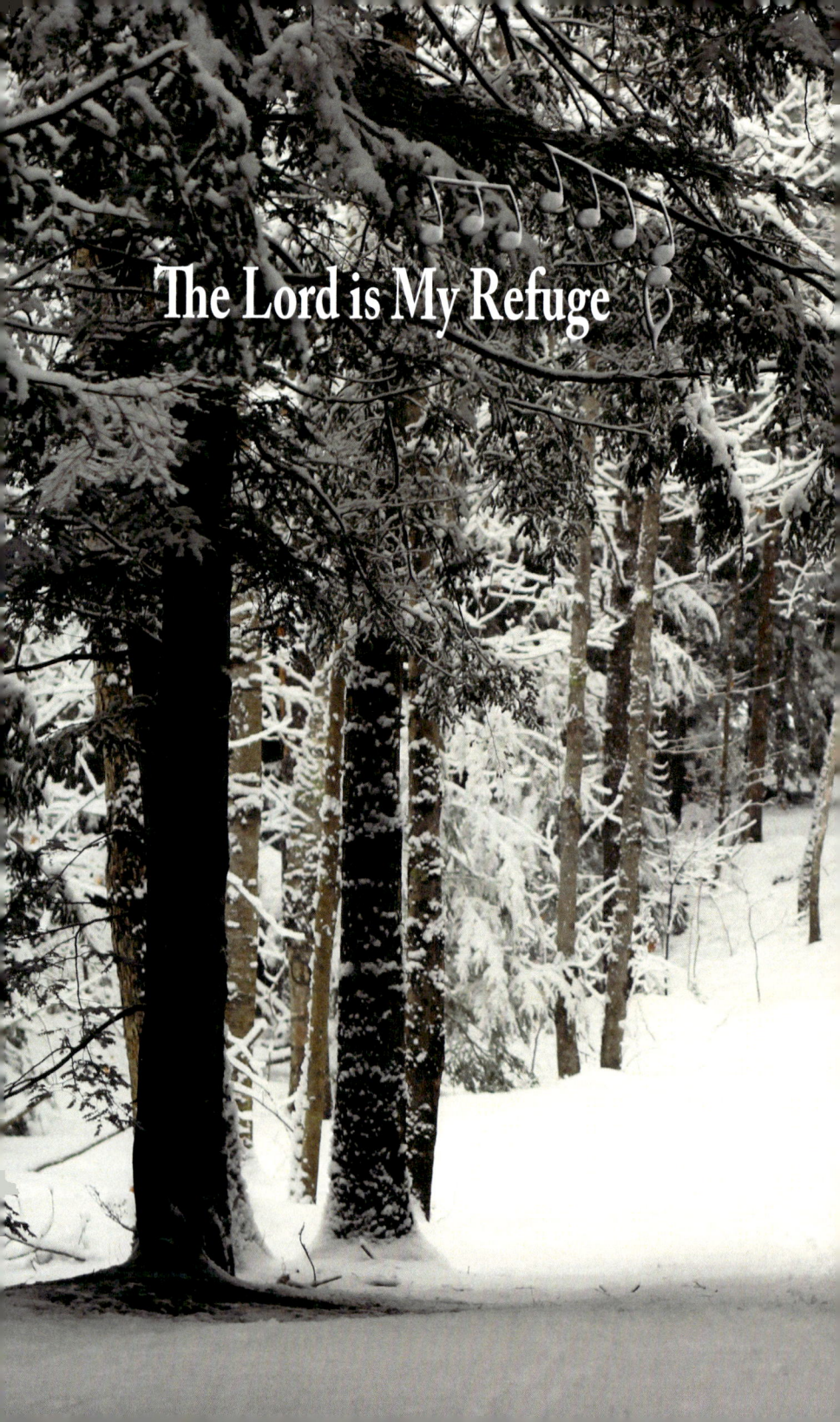

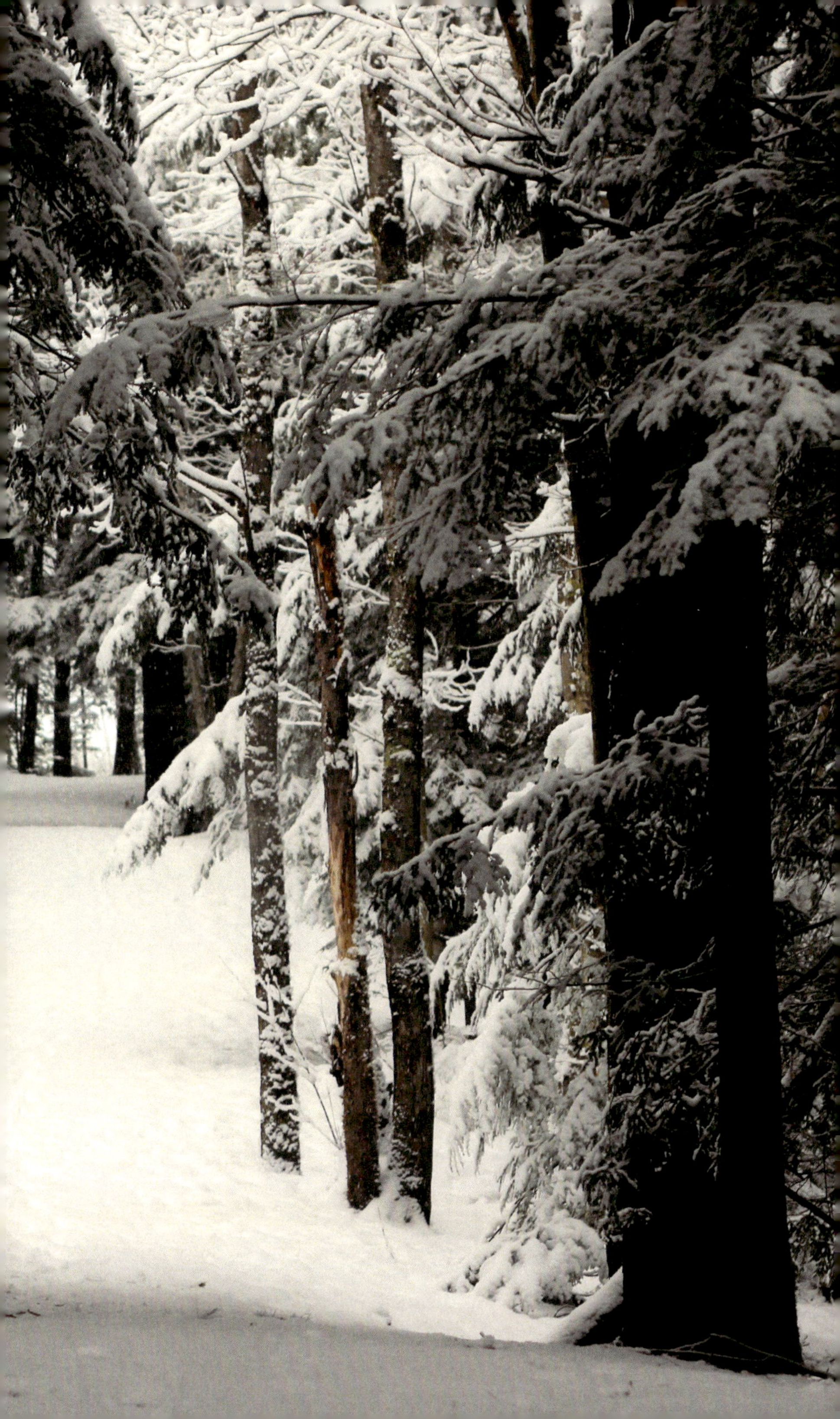

❦ Refuge ❦

The Lord is my Tower of Refuge;[1] I run to Him and am safe.[2] (*[1]Psalm 9:9-10. [2]Proverbs 18:10.*)

♪ I fear not what man can do,[3] for My Lord, the Eternal God, thunders through the heavens in my defense,[4] prepares me for battle and provides me with a full armor[5]—including brass shoes.[4] (*[3]Psalm 118:6. [4]Deuteronomy 33:25-28. [5]Psalm 18:9, 33-36.*)

♪ When I call upon Him, He delivers me,[6] dispels the darkness,[7] and gives me strength.[8] He is my refuge, not *from* evil, but *in the midst* of it.[9] (*[6]Psalm 50:15. [7]Psalm 18:28. [8]Psalm 59:16, 17. [9]2 Corinthians 11:18-27.*)

♪ His wings[10] are my shelter in the storm, shadow in the heat,[11] and refuge in the day of trouble.[12] He sends His angels to hold me up through pestilence, plague, and illness. Though ten thousand fall by my side, and arrows,[13] gunshots, and angry words fly in my face,[14] my confidence is not shaken,[15] for His everlasting arms are around me.[4] Though I be tempted, mocked, tortured, imprisoned or even slain, I am safe,[16] for I have made my Lord, even the Most High, my habitation.[17] ([10]*Psalm 91:1-4.* [11]*Isaiah 25:4.* [12]*Psalm 46:1-3.* [13]*Psalm 91:5-12.* [14]*Psalm 71:7-11.* [15]*Proverbs 14:26.* [16]*Hebrews 11:32-40.* [17]*Psalm 71:3.*)

♪ Through the power of His name,[1] I face whatever comes with praises on my lips[14] and songs in my heart,[18] for I have set my love upon Him.[19] ([18]*Psalm 59:16.* [19]*Psalm 91:14.*)

♪ Surely, I have hope,[20] for though I am surrounded by calamities, my salvation is sure,[21] and I shall stand beside the River of Life in the city of God.[22] ([20]*Hebrews 6:18, 19.* [21]*Psalm 91:15, 16.* [22]*Psalm 46:1-4.*)

I will say of the Lord, He is my refuge and my fortress: my God; in Him will I trust. Psalm 91:2

The Lord is My Judge

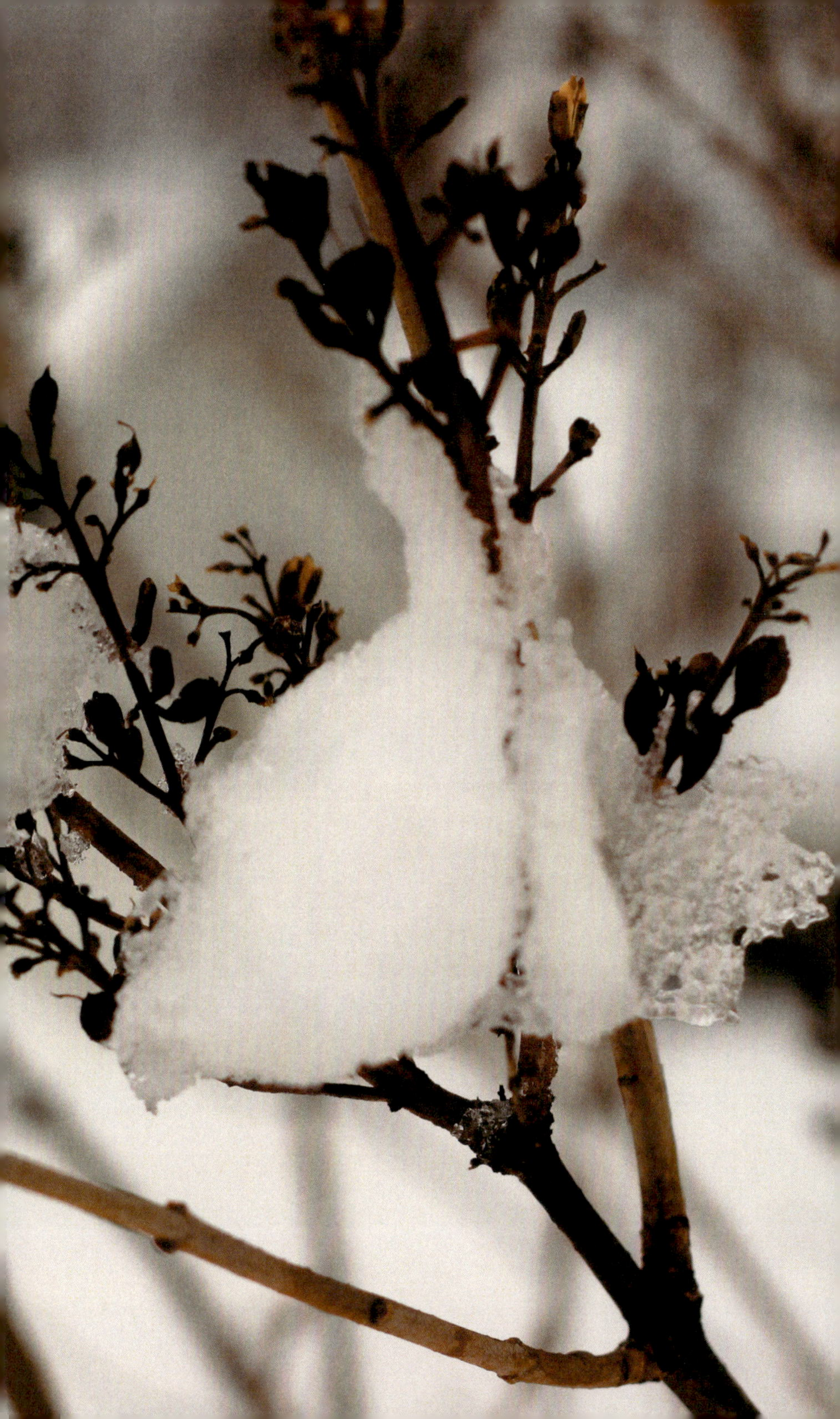

～ JUDGE ～

The Lord is my just[1] and holy[2] Judge;[3] Before Him, I am a sinner[4] and deserve to die.[5] *([1]John 5:30. [2]Revelation 15:4. [3]Isaiah 33:22. [4]Isaiah 6:5-7. [5]Romans 6:23.)*

♪ Yet He not only pardons my sins,[6] throws them into the depths of the sea,[7] washes them away,[8] and forgets them,[9] He leads me into truth and teaches me the way of salvation.[10] He takes my case into His hands[11] and gives me the words to say[12] so I can stand before my accuser without fear.[13] *([6]Isaiah 55:6-9. [7]Micah 7:18, 19. [8]Revelation 1:5. [9]Hebrews 8:12. [10]Psalm 25:5-11. [11]Psalm 89:13, 14. [12]Luke 12:11, 12. [13]Revelation 12:10.)*

♪ I will sing of His mercy[14] and grace,[15] for the consequences I suffer are less than I deserve.[16] I have rebelled, yet I am not consumed, for though I have disobeyed, He has not forsaken me.[17] *([14]Psalm 101:1. [15]Isaiah 30:18. [16]Ezra 9:13; Psalm 103:10. [17]Nehemiah 9:17, 30-33.)*

♪ The Lord is not only my Judge but also my Mediator,[18] my Advocate,[19] and my Intercessor.[20] He is my Refuge from oppression, trouble,[21] and deceitful and unjust people.[22] ([18]1 Timothy 2:5, 6. [19]1 John 2:1. [20]Romans 8:34. [21]Psalm 9:8, 9. [22]Psalm 43:1, 2.)

♪ I rejoice and am glad, for although my judge is high above the earth,[23] He loves righteousness and justice.[24] He has shown me His goodness, and I am thankful![23] ([23]Psalm 97:8-12. [24]Psalm 33:5.)

♪ Surely the day is coming when all who ever lived will bow before Him in worship,[25] for He will judge the earth in righteousness.[26] He will arise,[27] take vengeance upon the wicked,[28] destroy those who destroy the earth,[29] right all wrong,[30] vindicate His name,[31] cast down my accuser,[32] eliminate evil,[33] and gather His people unto Himself.[34] ([25]Romans 14:9-11. [26]Psalm 96:12-13. [27]Psalm 82:8. [28]Psalm 94:1, 2. [29]Revelation 11:18. [30]2 Peter 3:7; Jude 15, 16; Revelation 19:2. [31]Romans 3:1-26; Revelation 14:1-5; 1 Corinthians 4:9. [32]Revelation 12:10. [33]Psalm 58:10, 11. [34]Hebrews 9:27, 28; Revelation 21:26, 27.)

Fear God, and give glory to Him; for the hour of His judgment is come: and worship Him that made heaven, and earth, and the sea, and the fountains of waters.
REVELATION 14:6

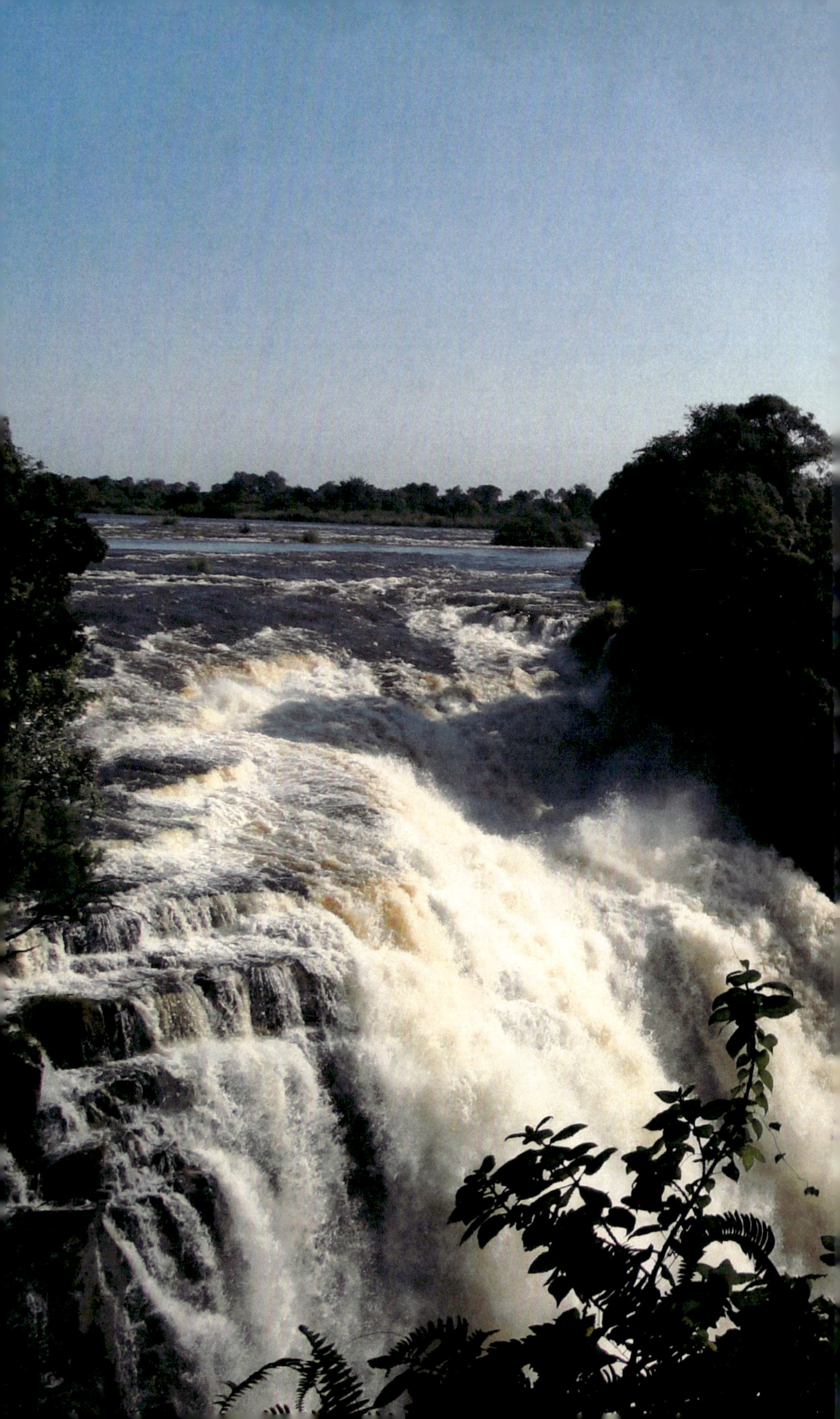

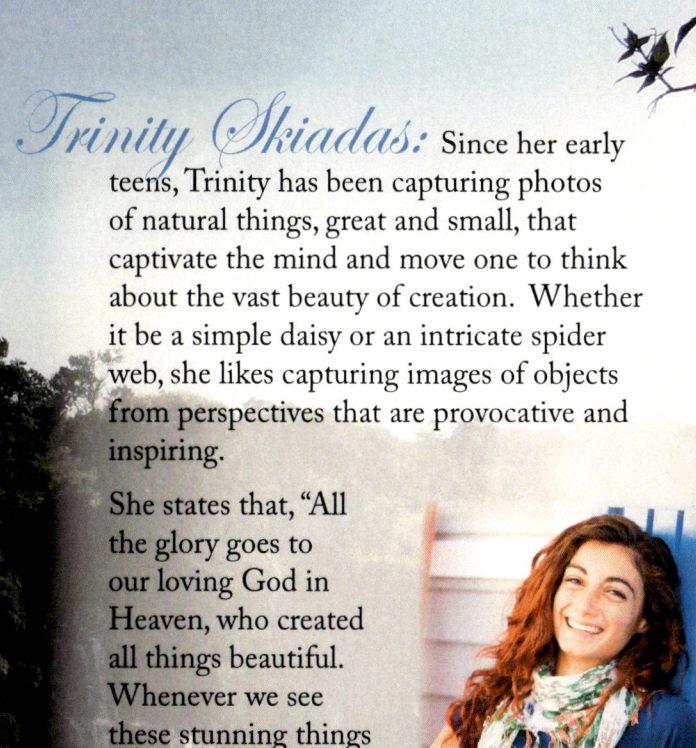

Trinity Skiadas: Since her early teens, Trinity has been capturing photos of natural things, great and small, that captivate the mind and move one to think about the vast beauty of creation. Whether it be a simple daisy or an intricate spider web, she likes capturing images of objects from perspectives that are provocative and inspiring.

She states that, "All the glory goes to our loving God in Heaven, who created all things beautiful. Whenever we see these stunning things He's made for us, we think of Him."

Trinity is pursuing a career that will enable her to touch people with God's love.

Trinity took this photo of Victoria Falls, Zimbabwe, during her visit to the Zimbabwe Orphanage Project. Most of the other photos in this book were taken in Maine, USA.

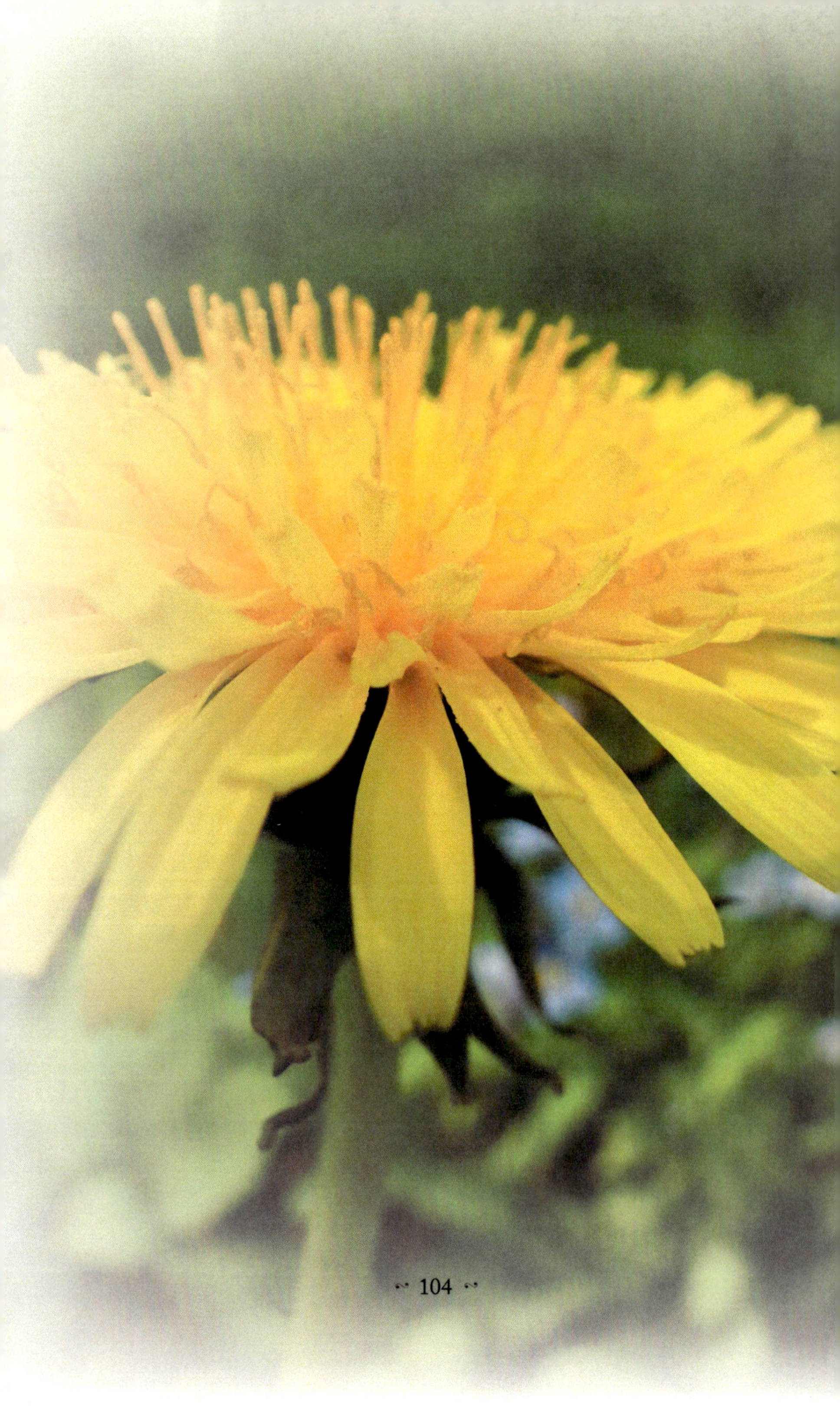

Beverly Koester credits her love and knowledge of the Bible to her father's nightly reading of the scriptures, her mother's encouragement to memorize Bible verses, Christian education and its emphasis on knowing and believing Bible doctrines, and to the late Elder Glenn Coon and his presentations on the ABC's of Bible prayer.

She had the privilege of helping get thousands of Bibles into eager hands during her African mission service of over 14 years. In Malawi she developed a Bible sales program to assist students in earning school fees. In Uganda and Sudan she assisted in the development of Adventist World Radio's Message of Hope and Bible correspondent school, which reached into South Sudan and served over 10,000 students in the first three years of operation.

"There are times," Beverly says, "when the ebb and flow of life leaves me too busy for serious study. Even then the Words of Scripture hidden in my heart *(Psalm 119:11)* carry me." She says that her most recent dive into scripture, through the writing of these psalms, has boosted her trust in the Lord and given her a new and exciting love for the Word of God.